# Other Books and Series by Jeff Bowen

*Applications for Enrollment of Chickasaw Newborn Act of 1905*
*Volumes I thru VII*

*Cherokee Intermarried White 1906 Volume I thru X*

*Applications for Enrollment of Creek Newborn Act of 1905*
*Volumes I thru XIV*

*Applications for Enrollment of Choctaw Newborn Act of 1905*
*Volume I, II, III, IV, V, VI, VII, VIII, IX, X, XI, XII, XIII, XIV, XV, XVI, XVII,*
*XVIII & XIX*

Visit our website at **www.nativestudy.com** to learn more about these
and other books and series by Jeff Bowen

I0209684

# APPLICATIONS FOR ENROLLMENT OF CHOCTAW NEWBORN ACT OF 1905

# VOLUME XX

TRANSCRIBED BY

# JEFF BOWEN

NATIVE STUDY
Gallipolis, Ohio
USA

# Other Books and Series by Jeff Bowen

*1901-1907 Native American Census  Seneca, Eastern Shawnee, Miami, Modoc, Ottawa, Peoria, Quapaw, and Wyandotte Indians  (Under Seneca School, Indian Territory)*

*1932 Census of The Standing Rock Sioux Reservation with Births And Deaths 1924-1932*

*Census of The Blackfeet, Montana, 1897- 1901  Expanded Edition*

*Eastern Cherokee by Blood, 1906-1910, Volumes I thru XIII*

*Choctaw of Mississippi Indian Census 1929-1932 with Births and Deaths 1924-1931    Volume I*
*Choctaw of Mississippi Indian Census 1933, 1934 & 1937, Supplemental Rolls to 1934 & 1935 with Births and Deaths 1932-1938, and Marriages 1936-1938 Volume II*

*Eastern Cherokee Census Cherokee, North Carolina 1930-1939*
*Census 1930-1931 with Births And Deaths 1924-1931 Taken By Agent L. W. Page Volume I*
*Eastern Cherokee Census  Cherokee, North Carolina 1930-1939*
*Census 1932-1933 with Births And Deaths 1930-1932 Taken By Agent R. L. Spalsbury    Volume II*
*Eastern Cherokee Census Cherokee, North Carolina 1930-1939*
*Census 1934-1937 with Births and Deaths 1925-1938 and Marriages 1936 & 1938 Taken by Agents R. L. Spalsbury And Harold W. Foght Volume III*

*Seminole of Florida Indian Census, 1930-1940 with Birth and Death Records, 1930-1938*

*Texas Cherokees 1820-1839  A Document For Litigation 1921*

*Choctaw By Blood Enrollment Cards 1898-1914 Volumes I thru XVII*

*Starr Roll 1894  (Cherokee Payment Rolls)  Districts: Canadian, Cooweescoowee, and Delaware  Volume One*
*Starr Roll 1894 (Cherokee Payment Rolls) Districts: Flint, Going Snake, and Illinois   Volume Two*
*Starr Roll 1894 (Cherokee Payment Rolls) Districts: Saline, Sequoyah, and Tahlequah; Including Orphan Roll  Volume Three*

*Cherokee Intruder Cases  Dockets of Hearings 1901-1909  Volumes I & II*

*Indian Wills, 1911-1921  Records of the Bureau of Indian Affairs*
*Books One thru Seven;*
*Native American Wills & Probate Records 1911-1921*

# Other Books and Series by Jeff Bowen

*Turtle Mountain Reservation Chippewa Indians 1932 Census with Births & Deaths, 1924-1932*

*Chickasaw By Blood Enrollment Cards 1898-1914 Volume I thru V*

*Cherokee Descendants East An Index to the Guion Miller Applications Volume I*
*Cherokee Descendants West An Index to the Guion Miller Applications Volume II (A-M)*
*Cherokee Descendants West An Index to the Guion Miller Applications Volume III (N-Z)*

*Applications for Enrollment of Seminole Newborn Freedmen, Act of 1905*

*Eastern Cherokee Census, Cherokee, North Carolina, 1915-1922, Taken by Agent James E. Henderson*   Volume I (1915-1916)
Volume II (1917-1918)
Volume III (1919-1920)
Volume IV (1921-1922)

*Complete Delaware Roll of 1898*

*Eastern Cherokee Census, Cherokee, North Carolina, 1923-1929, Taken by Agent James E. Henderson*   Volume I (1923-1924)
Volume II (1925-1926)
Volume III (1927-1929)

*Applications for Enrollment of Seminole Newborn Act of 1905 Volumes I & II*

*North Carolina Eastern Cherokee Indian Census 1898-1899, 1904, 1906, 1909-1912, 1914 Revised and Expanded Edition*

*1932 Hopi and Navajo Native American Census with Birth & Death Rolls (1925-1931) Volume 1 - Hopi*
*1932 Hopi and Navajo Native American Census with Birth & Death Rolls (1930-1932) Volume 2 - Navajo*

*Western Navajo Reservation Navajo, Hopi and Paiute 1933 Census with Birth & Death Rolls 1925-1933*

*Cherokee Citizenship Commission Dockets 1880-1884 and 1887-1889 Volumes I thru V*

Originally published:
Baltimore, Maryland
2013


Reprinted by:

Native Study LLC
Gallipolis, OH
*www.nativestudy.com*
2020


Library of Congress Control Number: 2020918113

ISBN: 978-1-64968-112-6

*Made in the United States of America.*

This series is dedicated to the descendants of the
Choctaw newborn listed in these applications.

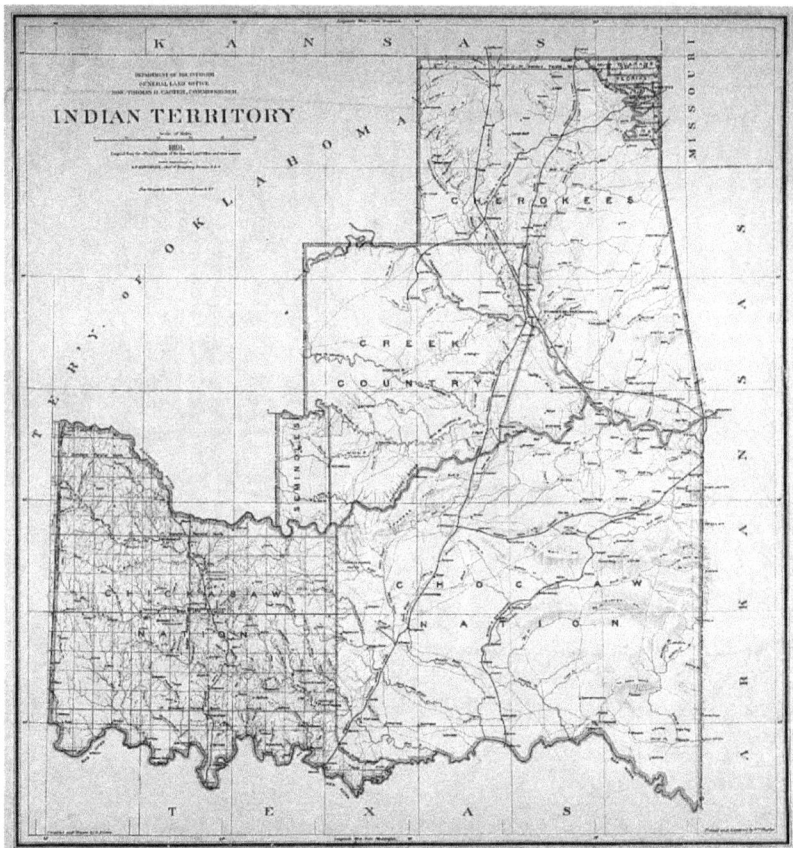

This map of Indian Territory shows how large the Choctaw and Chickasaw Nations' land base was that contained huge deposits of asphalt and coal. Just the size and territory involved was flooded with the "Grafters".

## Commissioner to the Five Civilized Tribes.

# NOTICE.

## Opening of Land Office at Wewoka,

### IN THE SEMINOLE NATION, INDIAN TERRITORY.

Notice is hereby given that on Monday, September 4, 1905, the Commissioner to the Five Civilized Tribes will establish a land office at Wewoka, in the Seminole Nation, Indian Territory, for the purpose of allowing citizens and freedmen of the Seminole Nation to select allotments of land for their minor children enrolled under the Act of Congress approved March 3, 1905 (33 Stat. L. 1060), and for the further purpose of allowing citizens and freedmen of the Seminole Nation, whose allotments are incomplete, to select additional land in order to bring the value of their allotments up to the standard of $309.09, as nearly as may be practicable.

Each child whose enrollment in accordance with the Act of March 3, 1905, has been duly approved by the Secretary of the Interior, is entitled to receive an alllotment of forty acres without regard to the character or value of the land selected.

Selection of allotments for minor children must be made by their citizen or freedmen parents or by a duly appointed guardian, or curator, or by a duly appointed administrator.

### TAMS BIXBY,
Commissioner.

Muskogee, Indian Territory,
July 29, 1905.

*This particular notice for the Seminole and Creek Newborn makes mention of the Act of 1905. It is likely that a similar notice was posted in the Choctaw and Chickasaw Nations for the registration of newborn children.*

DEPARTMENT OF THE INTERIOR,
## Commission to the Five Civilized Tribes.

### Rules and Regulations Governing the Selection of Allotments and the Designation of Homesteads in the Choctaw and Chickasaw Nations.

1. Selections of allotments and designations of homesteads for adult citizens and selections of allotments for adult freedmen must be made in person except as herein otherwise provided.

2. Applications to have land set apart and homesteads designated for duly identified Mississippi Choctaws must be made personally before the Commission to the Five Civilized Tribes. Fathers may apply for their minor children and if the father be dead the mother may apply. Husbands may apply for wives. Applications for orphans, insane persons and persons of unsound mind may be made by duly appointed guardian or curator, and for aged and infirm persons and prisoners by agents duly authorized thereunto by power of attorney, in the discretion of said Commission.

3. At the time of the selection of allotment each citizen and duly identified Mississippi Choctaw shall designate as a homestead out of said selection land equal in value to one hundred and sixty acres of the average allottable land of the Choctaw and Chickasaw Nations, as nearly as may be.

4. Each Choctaw and Chickasaw freedman, at the time of selection shall designate as his or her allotment of the lands of the Choctaw and Chickasaw Nations, land equal in value to forty acres of the average allottable land of the Choctaw and Chickasaw Nations.

5. Citizens, freedmen and identified Mississippi Choctaws who are married, whether they have attained their majority or not, will be regarded as of age for the purpose of making selections.

6. Selections may be made by citizen and freedman parents for unmarried male children under twenty-one years of age and for unmarried female children under eighteen years of age, and a male citizen or freedman may make selection for his wife, if she is entitled to make selection, unless she shall, at the time or previously thereto, protest in writing.

7. Where the father of an unmarried minor citizen, freedman or identified Mississippi Choctaw is a non-citizen, the citizen, freedman or identified Mississippi Choctaw mother of such children must make selection in person in behalf of said children.

8. Selections of allotments and designations of homesteads for minor citizens and selections of allotments for minor freedmen may be made by the citizen father or freedman father or mother, as the case may be, or by a guardian, curator, or an administrator having charge of their estate, in the order named.

9. Selections of allotments and designations of homesteads for citizen, and selections of allotment for freedmen, prisoners, convicts, aged and infirm persons and soldiers and sailors of the United States on duty outside of Indian Territory, may be made by duly appointed agents under power of attorney, and for incompetents by guardians, curators, or other suitable person akin to them.

10. Selections may be made and homesteads designated by duly identified Mississippi Choctaws, who have, within one year after the date of their identification as such, made satisfactory proof of bona fide settlement within the Choctaw-Chickasaw country, at any time within six months after the date of their said identification.

11. Persons authorized to make selections by power of attorney, as provided in rules 2 and 9 hereof, must be the husband or wife, or a relative not further removed than a cousin of the first degree of the person for whom such selection is made.

12. It shall be the duty of the Commission to the Five Civilized Tribes to see that selections of allotments and designations of homesteads for the classes of persons mentioned in rules 2, 6, 7, 8 and 9 hereof, are made for the best interests of such persons.

13. Selections of allotments for citizens, freedmen and identified Mississippi Choctaws who have died subsequent to September 25, 1902, and before making a selection of allotment, shall be made by a duly appointed administrator or executor. If, however, such administrator or executor be not duly and expeditiously appointed, or fails to act promptly when appointed, or for any other cause such selections be not so made within a reasonable and practicable time, the Commission to the Five Civilized Tribes shall designate the lands thus to be allotted.

14. In determining the value of a selection the appraised value of the land selected shall be increased by the appraised value of such pine timber on such land as has heretofore been estimated by the Commission to the Five Civilized Tribes.

15. Selections of allotments may be made only by citizens and freedmen whose enrollment has been approved by the Secretary of the Interior, and by persons duly identified by the Commission to the Five Civilized Tribes as Mississippi Choctaws, and by none others.

16. When a selection of land has been made by a citizen, freedman or identified Mississippi Choctaw, and the land so selected is claimed by a person whose rights as a citizen or freedman have not been finally determined, contest for the land so selected may be instituted by the person claiming the land, formal application for the land being first made as is required by the Rules of Practice in Choctaw and Chickasaw allotment contest cases.

THE COMMISSION TO THE FIVE CIVILIZED TRIBES.
Tams Bixby, Chairman.

Muskogee, Indian Territory, March 24, 1903.

The above statement published prior to 1905, was established for what was supposed to be a set of guidelines when it came to allotments. But with supplemental agreements and Congressional legislation, time frames as well as rules and regulations often changed and were not the same for every tribe.

# INTRODUCTION

The *Applications for Enrollment of Choctaw Newborn Act of 1905*, National Archive film M-1301, Rolls 50-57, are found under the heading of Applications for Enrollment of the Commission to the Five Civilized Tribes. For this series, I have transcribed the application forms filled out by individuals applying for enrollment in the Five Civilized Tribes under the Dawes Commission. These applications contain considerably more information than stated on the census cards found in series M-1186. M-1301 possesses its own numerical sequence, separate from M-1186. To find each party's roll number you would have to reference M-1186.

The Choctaw as well as the Chickasaw allotments were likely some of the most sought after properties in Indian Territory. There was supposed to be a 25-year restriction on the sale or lease of any Indian lands so as to insure that the owners wouldn't be swindled, but that isn't what happened. This fact is borne out in the Dawes Commission General Allotment Act, of February 8, 1887, Section 5, which "Provides that after an Indian person is allotted land, the United States will hold the land 'in trust [1] for the sole use and benefit of the Indian' (or his heirs if the Indian landowner dies) for a period of 25 years. (Land held in trust by the United States government cannot be sold or in anyway alienated by the Indian landowner, since the United States government considers the underlying ownership of the land held by itself and not the tribe. After the period of trust ends, the Indian landowner is free to sell the land and is free from any encumbrance from the United States.)"[1] Instead, Native Americans were exploited by the devious. The Choctaw and Chickasaw Districts both had huge asphalt and coal deposits, so there was pressure from outsiders to acquire them from the minute they were discovered. After repeated attacks throughout the years and many legislative changes, President "Roosevelt finally signed the Five Tribes Bill at noon on April 26, 1906, the forces seeking to end all restrictions were disappointed. Section 19 removed restrictions from the sale of all inherited land but directed that no full-bloods could sell their land for twenty-five years. The Act also prohibited leases for more than one year without the approval of the Secretary of the Interior."[2]

Angie Debo described the opportunists that wanted these Native American allotments as, "Grafters". The parents of the newborns enumerated within this series would no sooner receive the approval for their child's allotment than there would be someone there with cash in hand holding a new deed or lease for the parents to sign their child's birthright away. Angie Debo said it best, "As the business incapacity of the allottees became apparent, a horde of despoilers fastened themselves upon their property." According to Debo, "The term 'grafter' was applied as a matter of course to dealers in Indian land, and was frankly accepted by them. The speculative fever also affected Government employees so that it was almost impossible to prevent them from making personal investments."[3]

---

[1] General Allotment Act, Act of Feb. 8, 1887 (24 Stat. 388, ch. 119, 25 USCA 331)
[2] The Dawes Commission and the Allotment of the Five Civilized Tribes, 1893-1914 by Kent Carter, pg. 173
[3] And Still the Waters Run, Angie Debo, p. 92.

ix

# INTRODUCTION

According to the Department of Interior in 1905, "It is estimated that there will be added to the final rolls of the citizens and freedmen of the Choctaw and Chickasaw nations the names of 2,000 persons, including 1,500 new-born children to be enrolled under the provisions of the act of Congress approved March 3, 1905."[4]

The quote below explains, in detail, the requirements for qualifying as a newborn Choctaw, "By the act of Congress approved March 3, 1905 (H.R. 17474), entitled 'An act making appropriations for the current and contingent expenses of the Indian Department and for fulfilling treaty stipulations with various Indian tribes for the fiscal year ending June 30, 1906, and for other purposes,' it was provided as follows:

'That the Commission to the Five Civilized Tribes is hereby authorized for sixty days after the date of the approval of this act to receive and consider applications for enrollment of infant children born prior to September twenty-fifth, nineteen hundred and two, and who were living on said date, to citizens by blood of the Choctaw and Chickasaw tribes of Indians whose enrollment has been approved by the Secretary of the Interior prior to the date of the approval of this act; and to enroll and make allotments to such children.'

'That the Commission to the Five Civilized Tribes is authorized for sixty days after the date of the approval of this act to receive and consider applications for enrollment of children born subsequent to September twenty-fifth, nineteen hundred and two, and prior to March fourth, nineteen hundred and five, and who were living on said latter date, to citizens by blood of the Choctaw and Chickasaw tribes of Indians whose enrollment has been approved by the Secretary of the Interior prior to the date of the approval of this act; and to enroll and make allotments to such children.'

"Notice is hereby given that the Commission to the Five Civilized Tribes will, up to and inclusive of midnight, May 2, 1905, receive applications for the enrollment of infant children born prior to September 25, 1902, and who were living on said date, to citizens by blood of the Choctaw and Chickasaw tribes of Indians whose enrollment has been approved by the Secretary of the Interior prior to March 3, 1905."[5]

Following is the scope of these transcriptions: Besides the applications themselves, researchers will find the identities of other individuals within these applications -- doctors, lawyers, mid-wives, and other relatives -- that may help with you genealogical research.

Jeff Bowen
Gallipolis, Ohio
*NativeStudy.com*

---

[4] Annual Reports of the Department of the Interior For the Fiscal Year Ended June 30, 1905, p. 609.
[5] Annual Reports of the Department of the Interior For the Fiscal Year Ended June 30, 1905, p. 593.

Choc New Born 1479
    Thelmer Beal
    (Born April 8, 1905)

---

1479

# NEW BORN
## CHOCTAW
### ENROLLMENT

THELMER BEAL

(BORN APRIL 8, 1905)

As Citizen of the
CHOCTAW NATION
Act of Congress
Approved March 3, 1905

C A N C E L L E D

RECORD TRANSFERRED TO CHOCTAW

NEW BORN NO. 320

ACT OF CONGRESS APPROVED APRIL 26, 1906.

JULY 13, 1906

1479

---

# CHOCTAW   1479

# NEW BORN
ACT OF CONGRESS APPROVED MARCH 30, 1905.

*Thelmer Beaal*

*(Born April 8, 1905)*

1

# CANCELLED

*Record transferred to*
*Choctaw New Born No. 320.*
ACT OF CONGRESS APPROVED APRIL 26, 1906.

**JUL 13 1906**

---

Choc New Born 1480
    Clarence Bishop
    and
    Clara Bishop
    (Born Jan. 28, 1904)

**1480**

## NEW BORN
### CHOCTAW
### ENROLLMENT

CLARENCE BISHOP (AND)

CLARA BISHOP

(BORN JANUARY 28, 1904)

As Citizen of the
CHOCTAW NATION
Act of Congress
Approved March 3, 1905

C A N C E L L E D

RECORD TRANSFERRED TO CHOCTAW

NEW BORN NO. 708

ACT OF CONGRESS APPROVED APRIL 26, 1906.

JULY 13, 1906

**1480**

2

# CHOCTAW 1480

## NEW BORN

ACT OF CONGRESS APPROVED MARCH 30, 1905.

*Clarence Bishop (and)*
*Clara Bishop*
*(Born Jan. 28, 1904)*

# CANCELLED

*Record transferred to*
*Choctaw New Born No. 708.*
ACT OF CONGRESS APPROVED APRIL 26, 1906.

**JUL 13 1906**

Choc New Born 1481
    Jimmie Louise Braudrick
    (Born June 21, 1904)

1481

## NEW BORN
### CHOCTAW
### ENROLLMENT

JIMMIE LOUISE BRAUDRICK

(BORN JUNE 21, 1904)

As Citizen of the
CHOCTAW NATION
Act of Congress
Approved March 3, 1905

CANCELLED

3

RECORD TRANSFERRED TO CHOCTAW NEW BORN 376
ACT OF CONGRESS APPROVED APRIL 26, 1906.
JULY 13, 1906

### 1481

---

# CHOCTAW          1481

## NEW BORN

ACT OF CONGRESS APPROVED MARCH 30, 1905.

*Jimmie Louise Braudrick*

*(Born June 21, 1904)*

# CANCELLED

*Record transferred to*
*Choctaw New Born 376*

ACT OF CONGRESS APPROVED APRIL 26, 1906.

**JUL 13 1906**

---

Choc New Born 1482
    Georgia Ann Johnson
    (Born Nov. 17, 1903)

---

### 1482

## NEW BORN
### CHOCTAW
### ENROLLMENT

GEORGIA ANN JOHNSON

(BORN NOVEMBER 17, 1903)

WHITE CHILD

## Applications for Enrollment of Choctaw Newborn
## Act of 1905    Volume XX

As Citizen of the
CHOCTAW NATION
Act of Congress
Approved March 3, 1905

DECISION RENDERED JUNE 30, 1905

DECLINE TO RECEIVE OR CONSIDER JUNE 30, 1905
COPY OF DECISION FORWARDED ATTORNEYS FOR
CHOCTAW AND CHICKASAW NATIONS. JUNE 30, 1905
COPY OF DECISION FORWARDED APPLICANT'S
FATHER JUNE 30, 1905
RECORD FORWARDED DEPARTMENT JUNE 30, 1905
ACTION APPROVED BY SECRETARY OF INTERIOR
OCTOBER 21, 1905
NOTICE OF DEPARTMENTAL ACTION FORWARDED
ATTORNEYS FOR CHOCTAW AND CHICKASAW
NATIONS OCTOBER 31, 1905
NOTICE OF DEPARTMENTAL ACTION MAILED
APPLICANT'S FATHER OCTOBER 31, 1905

### 1482

_____

*(Copy)*

BIRTH AFFIDAVIT.

DEPARTMENT OF THE INTERIOR.
## COMMISSION TO THE FIVE CIVILIZED TRIBES.

_____

IN RE APPLICATION FOR ENROLLMENT, as a citizen of the        Choctaw        Nation, of
Georgia Ann Johnson         , born on the   17   day of Nov    , 1903

Name of Father:  George W Johnson            a citizen of the   Choctaw     Nation.
Name of Mother:  Nancy A. Johnson            a citizen of the   Choctaw     Nation.

Postoffice       Comanche, Ind. Ter.

_____

# Applications for Enrollment of Choctaw Newborn
## Act of 1905   Volume XX

UNITED STATES OF AMERICA, Indian Territory, ⎱
    Southern               DISTRICT. ⎰

    I,    Nancy A. Johnson     , on oath state that I am   28    years of age and a citizen by     intermarriage    , of the    Choctaw    Nation; that I am the lawful wife of George W Johnson          , who is a citizen, by   intermarriage    of the      Choctaw Nation; that a     female     child was born to me on   17   day of    November       , 1903; that said child has been named    Georgia Ann Johnson     , and was living March 4, 1905.

                          (Signed)    Nancy A. Johnson

Witnesses To Mark:

Subscribed and sworn to before me this   18   day of     April      , 1905

                   (Signed)   J. B. Wilkinson
                                Notary Public.

---

UNITED STATES OF AMERICA, Indian Territory, ⎱
    Southern               DISTRICT. ⎰

    I,    Charles Howell      , a    physician      , on oath state that I attended on Mrs.   Nancy A Johnson     , wife of    George W Johnson    on the   17   day of November    , 1903; that there was born to her on said date a    female    child; that said child was living March 4, 1905, and is said to have been named Georgia Ann Johnson

                          (Signed)   Dr. C.H. Howell

Witnesses To Mark:

Subscribed and sworn to before me this   18   day of     April      , 1905

                   (Signed)   J. B. Wilkinson
                                Notary Public.

---

*W.J.*

7-NB-1482.

### DEPARTMENT OF THE INTERIOR,
### COMMISSION TO THE FIVE CIVILIZED TRIBES.

In the matter of the application for the enrollment of Georgia Ann Johnson as a citizen by blood of the Choctaw Nation.

--D E C I S I O N :--

It appears from the record herein that on April 20, 1905 there was filed with the Commission application for the enrollment of Georgia Ann Johnson as a citizen of the Choctaw Nation.

It further appears from the record herein and the records of the Commission that the applicant was born November 17, 1903 and is a daughter of George W. Johnson, who is identified as G. W. Johnson, number 959 upon the final roll of citizens by intermarriage of the Choctaw Nation, and Nancy A. Johnson, who is an applicant to this Commission for enrollment as a citizen by intermarriage of the Choctaw Nation but whose right to such enrollment has not yet been determined.

The Act of Congress approved March 3, 1905 (Public No. 212) among other things provides:

"That the Commission to the Five Civilized Tribes is authorized for sixty days after the date of the approval of this act to receive and consider applications for enrollment of children born subsequent to September twenty-fifth, nineteen hundred and two, and prior to March fourth, nineteen hundred and five, and who were living on said latter date, to citizens by blood of the Choctaw and Chickasaw tribes of Indians whose enrollment has been approved by the Secretary of the Interior prior to the date of the approval of this act; and to enroll and make allotments to such children."

It is the opinion of this Commission that inasmuch as Georgia Ann Johnson is not a child of a citizen by blood of the Choctaw Nation of the Choctaw Nation the Commission is without authority to receive or consider the application for her enrollment as a citizen of the Choctaw Nation and that therefore the Commission should decline to receive or consider said application, under the provision of law above quoted, and it is so ordered.        COMMISSION TO THE FIVE CIVILIZED TRIBES,

> Tams Bixby
> Chairman.
> TB Needles
> Commissioner.
> C. R. Breckinbridge
> Commissioner.

Muskogee, Indian Territory.
JUN 30 1905

7-NB-1482

Muskogee, Indian Territory, June 30, 1905.

G. W. Johnson                                      **COPY**
    Comanche, Indian Territory.

Dear Sir:

Inclosed herewith you will find a copy of the decision of the Commission to the Five Civilized Tribes, rendered June 30, 1905, declining to receive or consider the application for the enrollment of Georgia Ann Johnson as a citizen of the Choctaw Nation.

The decision, with the record of proceedings in the case, is this day transmitted to the Secretary of the Interior for review. The final decision of the Secretary will be made known to you as soon as this office is informed of the same.

Respectfully,

SIGNED    *Tams Bixby*
Registered.                                      Chairman.
Incl. 7-NB-1482

———————

7-NB-1482

Muskogee,  Indian  Territory,
June 30, 1905.

Mansfield, McMurray & Cornish,                   **COPY**
    Attorneys for Choctaw and Chickasaw Nations,
        South McAlester, Indian Territory.

Gentlemen:

Inclosed herewith you will find a copy of the decision of the Commission to the Five Civilized Tribes, rendered June 30, 1905, declining to receive or consider the application for the enrollment of Georgia Ann Johnson as a citizen of the Choctaw Nation.

The decision, with the record of proceedings in the case, is this day transmitted to the Secretary of the Interior for review. The final decision of the Secretary will be made known to you as soon as this office is informed of the same.

8

## Applications for Enrollment of Choctaw Newborn
## Act of 1905   Volume XX

Respectfully,

ꞬꞋNꝹꞮꞄ   *Tams Bixby*

Chairman.

Incl. 7-NB-1482

---

Muskogee, Indian Territory, June 30, 1905.

The Honorable,                                        **COPY**
The Secretary of the Interior.

Sir:

There is herewith transmitted the record of proceedings in the matter of the application for the enrollment of Georgia Ann Johnson as a citizen by blood of the Choctaw Nation, including the decision of the Commission, dated June 30, 1905, declining to receive or consider said application.

Respectfully,
SIGNED

*Tams Bixby*

Through the                                           Chairman.
Commissioner of Indian Affairs.

2 Incl. 7-NB-1482.

---

DEPARTMENT OF THE INTERIOR,
OFFICE OF INDIAN AFFAIRS,
Land.                    WASHINGTON.          July 24, 1905.
50908-1905.

The Honorable,
The Secretary of the Interior

Sir:

I have the honor to enclose a report from the Commission to the Five Civilized Tribes, dated June 30, 1905, transmitting the record of the application for enrollment as a citizen of the Choctaw Nation of Georgia Ann Johnson.

June 30, 1905, the Commission decided adversely to the applicant.

The record shows that the applicant was born November 17, 1903, and is a daughter of George W. Johnson whose name appears at No. 959 upon the final roll of citizens by intermarriage of the Choctaw Nation approved by the Department August 20,

## Applications for Enrollment of Choctaw Newborn
## Act of 1905   Volume XX

1904, and Nancy A. Johnson an applicant for enrollment as a citizen by intermarriage of the Choctaw Nation, whose claim is pending.

In view of the record and of the act of March 3, 1905, (33 Stats., 1071) the approval of the Commission's decision adverse to the applicant is recommended.

Very respectfully,

C F Larrabee

M M M                                                            Acting Commissioner.
W

---

DEPARTMENT OF THE INTERIOR,

WASHINGTON.                GR

D C            48952-1905.                                       LLB
I T D          9084-1905.                  October 21, 1905.

LRS

Commissioner to the Five Civilized Tribes,
    Muskogee, Indian Territory.

Sir:

June 30, 1905, the Commission to the Five Civilized Tribes transmitted the record of the application made April 20, 1905, under the act of March 3, 1905, for the enrollment of Georgia Ann Johnson, an infant, born November 17, 1903, as a citizen by blood of the Choctaw Nation, including the decision of the Commission of same date, declining to receive or consider said application, on the ground that Georgia Ann Johnson is not a child of a citizen by blood of the Choctaw Nation and the Commission is therefore without authority to receive or consider the same.

July 24, 1905, the Acting Commissioner of Indian Affairs reporting thereon, recommended that the decision of the Commission, declining to receive or consider said application, be affirmed. A copy of his letter is inclosed.

The Department concurs in the recommendation made and the decision of the Commission to the Five Civilized Tribes dated June 30, 1905, declining to receive or consider said application on the ground that Georgia Ann Johnson is not a child of a citizen by blood of the Choctaw Nation is hereby affirmed.

Respectfully,

E. A. Hitchcock,

1 inclosure.                                                     Secretary.

---

7-NB-1482

Muskogee, Indian Territory, October 31, 1905.

G. W. Johnson,
Comanche, Indian Territory.

Dear Sir:

You are hereby notified that the Secretary of the Interior under date of October 21, 1905, affirmed the decision of the Commission to the Five Civilized Tribes, dated June 30, 1905, declining to receive or consider the application for the enrollment of Georgia Ann Johnson as a citizen of the Choctaw Nation.

Respectfully,

Commissioner.

---

7-NB-1482

Muskogee, Indian Territory, October 31, 1905.

Mansfield, McMurray & Cornish,
Attorneys for Choctaw and Chickasaw Nations,
South McAlester, Indian Territory.

Gentlemen:

You are hereby notified that the Secretary of the Interior under date of October 21, 1905, affirmed the decision of the Commission to the Five Civilized Tribes, dated June 30, 1905, declining to receive or consider the application for the enrollment of Georgia Ann Johnson as a citizen of the Choctaw Nation.

Respectfully,

Commissioner.

Choc New Born 1483
   Simeon D. Perkins
   (Born Oct. 20, 1903)
   Fannie Perkins
   (Born Jan. 29, 1905)

---

**BIRTH AFFIDAVIT.**
## DEPARTMENT OF THE INTERIOR.
## COMMISSION TO THE FIVE CIVILIZED TRIBES.

---

**IN RE APPLICATION FOR ENROLLMENT,** as a citizen of the ~~Summ~~ Chickasaw   Nation,
of   Simeon D.   , born on the   20  day of  Oct  , 1903

Name of Father: Joe Perkins         a citizen of the   Chickasaw  Nation.
Name of Mother: Addie Perkins      a citizen of the   Choctaw   Nation.

Postoffice    Filmore[sic] I.T.

---

**AFFIDAVIT OF MOTHER.**

**UNITED STATES OF AMERICA, Indian Territory,**⎫
   Southern District    **DISTRICT.**⎭

   I,  Addie Perkins   , on oath state that I am  21  years of age and a citizen
by   Blood   , of the   Choctaw   Nation; that I am the lawful wife of  Joe
Perkins, who is a citizen, by Blood   of the   Chickasaw   Nation; that a   male
child was born to me on  20   day of   Oct   , 1903; that said child has been named
Simeon D   , and was living March 4, 1905.

                     Addie Perkins
Witnesses To Mark:
    ⎧ Hannah Fillmore
    ⎩ Thomas Benton

   Subscribed and sworn to before me this  20  day of   Mar   , 1905

                J T Gardner
                Notary Public.

---

## Applications for Enrollment of Choctaw Newborn
## Act of 1905   Volume XX

### AFFIDAVIT OF ATTENDING PHYSICIAN OR MID-WIFE.

UNITED STATES OF AMERICA, Indian Territory, ⎫
Southern District      DISTRICT. ⎰

I,   Epsy Filmore      , a   Midwife      , on oath state that I attended on
Mrs.  Addie Perkins      , wife of   Joe Perkins      on the  20  day of   Oct    , 1903;
that there was born to her on said date a      male      child; that said child was living
March 4, 1905, and is said to have been named Simeon D.

                                             her
                                      Epsy  x  Filmore
Witnesses To Mark:                           mark
  ⎰ Hannah Fillmore
  ⎱ Thomas Benton

Subscribed and sworn to before me this  20  day of      Mar      , 1905

                            J T Gardner
                            Notary Public.

-----

BIRTH AFFIDAVIT.
### DEPARTMENT OF THE INTERIOR.
## COMMISSION TO THE FIVE CIVILIZED TRIBES.

-----

IN RE APPLICATION FOR ENROLLMENT, as a citizen of the      Chickasaw      Nation, of
Fany[sic]      , born on the   29  day of  Jan.   , 1905

Name of Father:  Joe Perkin                a citizen of the   Blood      Nation.
Name of Mother:  Addie Perkin              a citizen of the   Choctaw     Nation.

                  Postoffice      Filmore

-----

### AFFIDAVIT OF MOTHER.

UNITED STATES OF AMERICA, Indian Territory, ⎫
Southern District      DISTRICT. ⎰

I,   Addie Perkin      , on oath state that I am   21   years of age and a citizen by
Blood    , of the   Choctaw     Nation; that I am the lawful wife of   Joe Perkin, who is
a citizen, by  Blood     of the      Chickasaw      Nation; that a      male[sic]      child
was born to me on  29   day of   Jan.    , 1905; that said child has been named   Fany
, and was living March 4, 1905.

                            Addie Perkin

13

Witnesses To Mark:
  { Hannah Fillmore
  { Thomas Benton

Subscribed and sworn to before me this 20   day of      Mar       , 1905

J T Gardner
Notary Public.

---

### AFFIDAVIT OF ATTENDING PHYSICIAN OR MID-WIFE.

UNITED STATES OF AMERICA, Indian Territory, }
  Southern District        DISTRICT. }

I,   Epsy Filmore          , a    Midwife       , on oath state that I attended on
Mrs.  Addie Perkin       , wife of   Joe Perkin      on the 29   day of   Jan    , 1905;
that there was born to her on said date a      female      child; that said child was living
March 4, 1905, and is said to have been named   Fany

her
Epsy  x  Filmore
mark

Witnesses To Mark:
  { Hannah Fillmore
  { Thomas Benton

Subscribed and sworn to before me this 20   day of      Mar       , 1905

J T Gardner
Notary Public.

---

*(The below typed as given.)*

Southern Dist }
Ind. Ter      }   ss

To the Hon. Commissioner to the five Civilized Tribes.

This is to certify that on April 1st 1900, I united in matrimony as husband and wife Joseph Perkins and Addie Fronterhouse in the town of Emet, I.T. in the presence of these witnesses
L. J. Milburn and J. M. Roper.
Witness my signature on this the 22rd day of April 1905.

*M. H. Roper*
*Minister of Gospel.*
*Be it know that on this day appered M. H. Roper and acknowledged that the above statement was true and correct.*

*L. J. Milburn*
*Notary Public*

---

W. H. RITCHIE, President.
C. J. RALSTON, Vice-President.

R. R. HALL, Sect'y and Treas.
H. R. BROWN, Ass't Sect'y and Treas.

*(Illegible)* **OF CANEY.**

**CAPITAL STOCK, $50,000.**

Caney, J. J. _____ 190____

Dawes Commission
Muskogee I.T.
Gentlemen:

We the undersigned parents of Fannie Perkins hereby choose the Choctaw Nation as the one in which to file the land of said Fannie Perkins
Witness our hands & seals this the 19th day of June 1905 in Caney I.T.

Joe H Perkins
Addie Perkins

Subscribed & sworn to me this 19th day of June 1905

R.R. Hall

---

Ind Territory }
Southern Dist }

On this the 8th day of Aug 1905
Personally appeared before me

a Notary Public for the Southern Dist of the Ind Tery Joseph H Perkins a Chickasaw Indian by Blood and Addie Perkins a Choctaw Indian by Blood father and mother of Simeon D Perkins and state on oath that they desire to have their son Simeon D Perkins placed on the Choctaw rolls for enrollment.

In testimony where unto we have set our hand and seal this the 8th day of Aug 1905

Joseph H Perkins
Addie Perkins

15

*Subscribed and sworn to before me this sworn to before me this the 8th day of Aug 1905*

*R F French*

*Notary Public*

*My commission expires 1st day of June 1907*

---

BIRTH AFFIDAVIT.

### DEPARTMENT OF THE INTERIOR.
### COMMISSION TO THE FIVE CIVILIZED TRIBES.

---

IN RE APPLICATION FOR ENROLLMENT, as a citizen of the    Chickasaw    Nation, of
Fannie Perkins         , born on the   29th   day of   January  , 1905

Name of Father: Joe Perkins          a citizen of the   Chickasaw  Nation.
Name of Mother: Addie Perkins          a citizen of the   Choctaw    Nation.

Postoffice    Fillmore IT

---

AFFIDAVIT OF MOTHER.

UNITED STATES OF AMERICA, Indian Territory, ⎤
  Southern           DISTRICT. ⎦

I,   Addie Perkins      , on oath state that I am    21    years of age and a citizen
by     blood    , of the    Choctaw    Nation; that I am the lawful wife of   Joe Perkins,
who is a citizen, by  blood     of the        Chickasaw       Nation; that a      Female
child was born to me on   29th    day of    January     , 1905; that said child has been
named   Fannie    , and was living March 4, 1905.

Addie Perkins

Witnesses To Mark:

{

Subscribed and sworn to before me this  12   day of     Aug     , 1905

J T Gardner
Notary Public.

---

16

# Applications for Enrollment of Choctaw Newborn
## Act of 1905  Volume XX

### AFFIDAVIT OF ATTENDING PHYSICIAN OR MID-WIFE.

UNITED STATES OF AMERICA, Indian Territory, ⎱
   Southern            DISTRICT. ⎰

I,    Epsy Filmore      , a    midwife     , on oath state that I attended on Mrs. Addie Perkins    , wife of   Joe Perkins    on the  29th  day of    January    , 1905; that there was born to her on said date a     Female     child; that said child was living March 4, 1905, and is said to have been named    Fannie

her

Epsy x Filmore

mark

Witnesses To Mark:
   ⎰ *(Name Illegible)*
   ⎰ Jannette Filmore

Subscribed and sworn to before me this  12  day of     Aug     , 1905

J T Gardner

Notary Public.

_____

9-1693

Muskogee, Indian Territory, March 25, 1905.

Joe Perkins,
     Filmore, Indian Territory.

Dear Sir:

     Receipt is hereby acknowledged of the affidavits of Addie Perkins and Epsy Filmore to the birth of Simeon D. and Fannie Perkins, children of Joe and Addie Perkins, October 20, 1903, and January 29, 1905, respectively, and the same have been filed with our records as an application for the enrollment of said child.

Respectfully,

Chairman.

_____

# Applications for Enrollment of Choctaw Newborn
## Act of 1905   Volume XX

9 N B 243

Muskogee, Indian Territory, April 15, 1905.

Joe Perkins,
    Fillmore, Indian Territory,

Dear Sir:

You are hereby advised that before the applications for the enrollment of your infant children, Simeon D. Perkins, and Fany Perkins, can be finally disposed of, it will be necessary for you to furnish the Commission with either the original or a certified copy of the license and certificate of your marriage to their mother, Addie Perkins.

Please give this matter your immediate attention.

Respectfully,

Chairman.

---

9 NB 243

Muskogee, Indian Territory, April 26, 1905.

Joe Perkins,
    Fillmore, Indian Territory,

Dear Sir:

Receipt is hereby acknowledged of the affidavit of M. H. Roper to the marriage of Joseph Perkins and Addie Fronterhouse, and the same has been filed with the record in the matter of the enrollment of your child.

Respectfully,

Chairman.

---

9-NB-243.

Muskogee, Indian Territory, May 15, 1905.

Joe Perkin[sic],
    Fillmore, Indian Territory,

Dear Sir:

Referring to the application for the enrollment of your infant child, Fany Perkin, it appears that you are a citizen by blood of the Chickasaw Nation, while your wife is a citizen by blood of the Choctaw Nation.

Your attention is called to the provision of The Act of Congress approved June 28, 1898, as follows:

The several Tribes may, by agreement, determine the right of persons who for any reason may claim citizenship in two or more tribes, and to allotment of lands and distribution of moneys belonging to each tribe; but if no such agreement be made, then such claimant shall be entitled to such rights in one tribe only, and may elect in which tribe he will take such right; but if he fail or refuse to make such selection in due time, he shall be enrolled in the tribe with whom he has resided, and there be given such allotment and distributions, and not elsewhere.

It will therefore be necessary for you and your wife to appear before a Notary Public or other officer authorized to administer oaths and by affidavit elect in which nation you desire to have said child enrolled, forwarding same, when properly executed, to the Commission.

Respectfully,

Chairman.

-------------

9-NB-243

Muskogee, Indian Territory, June 21, 1905.

Joe Perkins,
    Filmore, Indian Territory.

Dear Sir:

Receipt is hereby acknowledged of the joint affidavit of yourself and your wife Addie Perkins electing to have your child Fannie Perkins enrolled as a citizen by blood of the Choctaw Nation and the same has been filed with the record in the matter of the enrollment of said child.

Respectfully,

Chairman.

---

9-NB-243

Muskogee, Indian Territory, July 21, 1905.

Joe Perkins,
Fillmore, Indian Territory,

Dear Sir:

Referring to the application for the enrollment of your infant children, Simeon D. Perkins and Fany Perkins, it appears that you are a citizen by blood of the Chickasaw Nation, and that you wife is a citizen by blood of the Choctaw Nation.

Your attention is called to the following provision of The Act of Congress approved June 28, 1898:

"The several Tribes may, by agreement, determine the right of persons who for any reason may claim citizenship in two or more tribes, and to allotment of lands and distribution of moneys belonging to each tribe; but if no such agreement be made, then such claimant shall be entitled to such rights in one tribe only, and may elect in which tribe he will take such right; but if he fail or refuse to make such selection in due time, he shall be enrolled in the tribe with whom he has resided, and there be given such allotment and distributions, and not elsewhere."

It appears on June 21, 1905, you filed the affidavit of yourself and your wife electing Choctaw enrollment for your child, Fany Perkins, but did not include the name of your child, Simeon D. Perkins, in said affidavit. It will, therefore, be necessary for you and your wife to appear before a Notary Public or other officer authorized to administer oaths and prepare affidavits electing in which Nation you desire to have your child, Simeon D. Perkins, enrolled, forwarding same when properly executed, to this office.

Respectfully,

Commissioner.

---

# Applications for Enrollment of Choctaw Newborn
## Act of 1905    Volume XX

7-NB-1483

Muskogee, Indian Territory, August 4, 1905.

Joe Perkins,
Fillmore, Indian Territory,

Dear Sir:

There is inclosed you herewith for execution application for the enrollment of your infant child, born January 29, 1905.

In the affidavit of March 20, 1905, heretofore filed in this office, the affidavit of the mother gives the name of the said child as "Fany", and the sex as "male"; in the affidavit of the midwife, executed the same date, the name is given as "Fany", and the sex as "female"; in the joint affidavit of yourself and wife, executed June 19, 1905, the name is given as "Fannie."

In the inclosed application, the name and sex is left blank. Please insert the correct name and sex and have the affidavits properly executed and return to this office immediately, as no further action can be taken relative to the enrollment of your said child, until the evidence requested is supplied.

Respectfully,

LM 5/4                                                                        Commissioner.

-------------------------

7-NB-1483

Muskogee, Indian Territory, August 9, 1905.

Joe Perkins,
Filmore, Indian Territory.

Dear Sir:

Receipt is hereby acknowledged of the joint affidavit of Joseph H. and Addie Perkins, electing to have your child Simeon D. Perkins enrolled as a citizen by blood of the Choctaw Nation and the same has been filed with the record in this case.

Respectfully,

Acting Commissioner.

-------------------------

7-NB-1483

Muskogee, Indian Territory, August 15, 1905.

Joe Perkins,
    Filmore, Indian Territory.

Dear Sir:

Receipt is hereby acknowledged of the affidavits of Addie Perkins and Epsy Filmore, to the birth of Fannie Perkins daughter of Joe and Addie Perkins, January 29, 1905, and the same are returned you herewith for the reason that the Notary Public before whom the affidavits were acknowledged has neglected to affix his notarial seal thereto. Please have the seal of the Notary affixed to these affidavits and return them to this office as early as possible.

Respectfully,

LM 5/4                                                          Acting Commissioner.

---

7-NB-1483.

Muskogee, Indian Territory, August 21, 1905.

Joe Perkins,
    Filmore, Indian Territory.

Dear Sir:

Receipt is hereby acknowledged of the affidavits of Addie Perkins and Epsy Filmore as to the birth of your daughter Fannie Perkins on January 29, 1905, and the same have been filed in the matter of the application for the enrollment of said child as a citizen by blood of the Choctaw Nation.

Respectfully,

Commissioner.

<u>Choc New Born 1484</u>
> Ruby Gertrude Crawford
> (Born Oct. 18, 1902)

_____

*(Below typed as given.)*

Friday March 18th 1904                    March Term    1904

Court Met pursuant to adjournment present and presiding Hon. Wm H H Clayton Judge of the United States Court for the Central District of the Indian Territory. Whereupon the following proceedings were had to-wit:-

Barnet Crawford        plaintiff,
    vs
Minnie Crawford        Defendant

On the 18th day of March 1904, the time being a day of the regular March 1904 Term of said court, came on to be heard the above entitled cause the plaintiff appearing by his attorney J V Connell and the defendant wholly making default. And the court finding that the defendant had been duely served and legally summoned by a waiver of service herein:

And, the court further finding, from the reading of the evidence, that the allegations of abandonment, set out in plaintiff's complaint had been establishe according to law, that the release paryed for should be granted; it is therefore considered ordered and adjudged by the court that the bonds of matrimony heretofore existing between Barnet Crawford and Minnie Crawford be and the same are hereby canceled, set aside and held for naught.

And each party hereto be restored to all property not disposed of at the beginning of this action which either received of or from the other during the marriage or by reason thereof.

I, E.J.Fannin Clerk of the U S Court do hereby certify the above to be a true and correct copy of the record entry in the above styled couse as the same appears of record in my office at Durant I.T.

Given under my hand and the seal of the Court at Durant on this the 7th day of August 1905

> E.J.Fannin      Clerk
> By  *(Name Illegible)*      Deputy

_____

*Mr* Barney Crawford

AND

*M* Minnie Burnes.

# Marriage Certificate

DEPARTMENT OF THE INTERIOR,
COMMISSION TO THE FIVE CIVILIZED TRIBES.
**FILED**

MAY 1- 1905

*Tams Bixby* CHAIRMAN.

*Issued* March 15th *1*905.

Pat Henry *Clerk*

*By* Henry Wells *Deputy*

## Marriage Certificate

STATE OF
TEXAS

COUNTY OF
Fannin

*This Instrument Witnesseth that on the* **17th**
*day of* **May** *A.D. 1* **899** *there was issued out of the office
of the Clerk of the County Court of said County a License for
the Marriage of*

24

*Mr* **Barney Crawford**

*and Miss* **Minnie Burnes**

*and on the* 28th *day of* May *A.D.* 1899 *said parties were legally united in Marriage by a properly authorized person, named in said License and due return thereof made to this office in the manner and form required by law, all of which is duly entered upon the Marriage Records of my office in Vol* L *Page* 361

𝔚𝔦𝔱𝔫𝔢𝔰𝔰 *my hand and official seal at my office in* Benham *Texas on this the* 15th *day of* March *A.D.* 1905.

> **Pat Henry**
> *Clerk County Court* **Fannin** *County Texas*
> *By* **Henry Wells**
> *Deputy*

---

*Central Judicial District*
*Indian Territory*

I, J. S. Durant after having been first duly sworn state - I am about 40 years old and reside at Benington[sic], Indian Territory. I am the husband of Minnie Durant who was formerly the wife of Barny Crawford. We were married under a United States Court license on the 6th day of February 1905.

I am acquainted with her small daughter Ruby Gertrud Crawford. She is alive and is living with us here at Benington, I.T. at our house.

*J. S. Durant*

Subscribed and sworn to before me this the 22nd day of April 1905
*L. D. Horton*
*Notary Public*

---

25

*Central District*

*ss*

*Indian Territory*

I Minnie Durant, Indian Territory after having been first duly sworn state - I am the identical Minnie Durant whose maiden name was Minnie Burns and who married Barnett Crawford in May 1899 and am the mother of Ruby Gertrud Crawford, the issue of said marriage born October 18th 1902. And for whose enrollment I have made an application (7-3619.)

Barnett Crawford, my first husband aforesaid has been called Barney Crawford and I forgot to tell the Notary Public of this when he made the application - He is a Choctaw by blood and his Roll number is 14370 - His homestead certificate is No. 658 and his Surplus Certificate is No. 548.

He lives at Wade, I.T. and is married to another woman, her name was Lizzie Jolly. He is now 23 years old and his father is called George and his mother, now dead was called Talithia. His father

*(End of affidavit)*

---

BIRTH AFFIDAVIT.

## DEPARTMENT OF THE INTERIOR.
## COMMISSION TO THE FIVE CIVILIZED TRIBES.

---

**IN RE APPLICATION FOR ENROLLMENT,** as a citizen of the      Choctaw      Nation, of
Rubie Gertrude Crawford      , born on the  18  day of  October   , 1902

Name of Father: Barney Crawford                    a citizen of the   Choctaw     Nation.
*who was formerly*
Name of Mother: Minnie Durant  *Minnie Crawford* a citizen of the   Choctaw     Nation.

Postoffice      Bennington, I.T.

---

AFFIDAVIT OF MOTHER.

UNITED STATES OF AMERICA, Indian Territory,
Central Judicial          DISTRICT.

I, Minnie Durant *(Formerly Minnie Crawford)* , on oath state that I am   21   years of age and a citizen by      nativity    , of the    United States    Nation; that I am the

26

lawful wife of   J. S. Durant *(I was the wife of Barny Crawford Oct. 18th 1902 and from whom I am now lawfully divorced* , who is a citizen, by blood   of the   Choctaw   Nation; that a   female   child was born to me on   18   day of   October   , 1902; that said child has been named   Ruby Gertrude Crawford   , and was living March 4, 1905.

                                                              Minnie Durant
Witnesses To Mark:                                *Formerly Minnie Crawford*

{

        Subscribed and sworn to before me this  22  day of     April     , 1905

                                          L.D. Horton
                                          Notary Public.

                                  _____

                                                        7--3619.

                              Muskogee, Indian Territory, May 8, 1905.

Minnie Durant,
        Bennington, Indian Territory.

Dear Madam:

        Receipt is hereby acknowledged of the affidavits of J. S. Durant, Indian Territory Minnie Durant (Crawford) and V. T. Stephens to the birth of Ruby Gertrude Crawford, daughter of Barney and Minnie Crawford, October 18, 1902.   Receipt is also acknowledged of the marriage license and certificate between Barney Crawford and Minnie Burnes.

        It is stated in the affidavits that Barney Crawford is a citizen by blood of the Choctaw Nation, and in order to enable us to identify him upon our records you are requested to state his age, the names of his parents and such other information as will enable us to identify him upon our records as an enrolled citizen by blood of the Choctaw Nation.

        This matter should receive immediate attention.

                                          Respectfully,

                                                  Commissioner in Charge.

                                  _____

# Applications for Enrollment of Choctaw Newborn
## Act of 1905   Volume XX

*Substitute*

7-NB-1484.

Muskogee, Indian Territory, June 27, 1905.

Minnie Durant,
  Bennington, Indian Territory.

Dear Madam:

Referring to the application for the enrollment of your infant child, Ruby Gertrude Crawford, born October 18, 1902, it is noted from the affidavits heretofore filed in this office that you are now the wife of J. S. Durant; that at the time of the birth of the applicant you were the wife of Barney Crawford, from whom you have been divorced.

In this event it will be necessary for you to file in this office, either the original or a certified copy of the decree of divorce between you and Barney Crawford.

Please give this matter your immediate attention as no further action can be taken in this case until this evidence is filed.

Respectfully,

Chairman.

---

7-NB-1484

Muskogee, Indian Territory, July 28, 1905.

Minnie Durant,
  Bennington, Indian Territory,

Dear Madam:

Referring to the application for the enrollment of your infant child, Ruby Gertrude Crawford, born October 18, 1902, it appears from the evidence of the mother, offered in support of such application that you were divorced from your former husband, Barnett Crawford, and are now the wife of J. S. Durant.

Before any further action can be taken relative to the enrollment of your said child, it will be necessary that you file in this office a certified copy of the divorce proceedings from your former husband, Barnett Crawford.

This matter should receive your immediate attention.

Respectfully,

Commissioner.

28

---

7-3697
7-NB-1484

Muskogee, Indian Territory, August 4, 1905.

L. D. Horton,
   Attorney at Law,
      Boswell, Indian Territory.

Dear Sir:

Receipt is hereby acknowledged of your letter of July 29, 1905, enclosing affidavits to the birth and death of Eunice Battiest, born October 23, 1901, and died June 8, 1904, and the same have been filed in the matter of the enrollment of said child.

Replying to that portion of your letter in which you ask if anything further is necessary in the matter of the enrollment of Ruby Gertrude Crawford you are advised that on July 28, 1905, a letter was addressed to Minnie Durant, Bennington, Indian Territory, informing her that it would be necessary for her to furnish a certified copy of the decree of divorce from her former husband Barney Crawford, but this evidence has not yet been received.

Respectfully,

Commissioner.

---

7-NB-1484

Muskogee, Indian Territory, August 11, 1905.

L. D. Horton,
   Boswell, Indian Territory.

Dear Sir:

Receipt is hereby acknowledged of your letter of August 8, 1905, transmitting copy of the decree of divorce between Barnett and Minnie Crawford which you offer in support of the application of Ruby Gertrude Crawford for enrollment as a citizen by blood of the Choctaw Nation and the same has been filed with the record in this case.

Respectfully,

Acting Commissioner.

---

# Applications for Enrollment of Choctaw Newborn
## Act of 1905   Volume XX

7-NB-1484

Muskogee, Indian Territory, October 30, 1905.

J. S. Durant,
Bennington, Indian Territory.

Dear Sir:

Receipt is hereby acknowledged of your letter of October 24, 1905, asking if you can file for Ruby Girtie[sic] Crawford.

In reply to your letter you are advised that on September 23, 1905, the Secretary of the Interior approved the enrollment of Ruby Gertrude Crawford, child of Barnett Crawford and Minnie Durant as a citizen by blood of the Choctaw Nation and selection of allotment may now be made in her behalf in accordance with the rules and regulations governing the selection of allotments and the designation of homesteads in the Choctaw and Chickasaw Nations.

Respectfully,

Commissioner.

---

7-NB-1484

Muskogee, Indian Territory, June 4, 1906.

L. D. Horton,
Attorney at Law,
Durant, Indian Territory.

Dear Sir:

Receipt is hereby acknowledged of your letter of May 22, 1906, asking if there is now any method of securing the enrollment of Minnie Durant, formerly Minnie Crawford, whos[sic] is now the wife of J. S. Durant.

In reply to your letter you are advised that it does not appear from the records of this office that application has been made by or on behalf of Minnie Durant for enrollment as an intermarried citizen of the Choctaw Nation either under the name of Minnie Durant, or Minnie Crawford, and under existing legislation, there is no provision for the reception of original applications for enrollment in the Choctaw or Chickasaw Nations[sic].

Respectfully,

Commissioner.

Choc New Born 1485
>   Motsy Gibson
>   (Born Nov. 24, 1904)

---

BIRTH AFFIDAVIT.

### DEPARTMENT OF THE INTERIOR.
## COMMISSION TO THE FIVE CIVILIZED TRIBES.

---

**IN RE APPLICATION FOR ENROLLMENT,** as a citizen of the     Choctaw     Nation, of
Motsy Gibson        , born on the  24th   day of  November   , 1904

Name of Father:     Morris Gibson          a citizen of the   Choctaw     Nation.
Name of Mother:     Melissa Gibson         a citizen of the   Choctaw     Nation.

Postoffice     Antlers, Ind. Ter.

---

**AFFIDAVIT OF MOTHER.**

UNITED STATES OF AMERICA, Indian Territory, ⎫
    Central                DISTRICT. ⎭

I,   Melissa Gibson    , on oath state that I am   24    years of age and a citizen
by     blood    , of the     Choctaw     Nation; that I am the lawful wife of   Morris
Gibson        , who is a citizen, by  blood    of the     Choctaw     Nation; that a
female     child was born to me on   24th   day of   November    , 1904; that said
child has been named   Motsy Gibson      , and was living March 4, 1905.

Melissa Gibson

Witnesses To Mark:
    ⎰

Subscribed and sworn to before me this  1st  day of    May     , 1905

Wirt Franklin
Notary Public.

---

**AFFIDAVIT OF ATTENDING PHYSICIAN OR MID-WIFE.**

UNITED STATES OF AMERICA, Indian Territory, ⎫
    Central                DISTRICT. ⎭

I,   Agnes Billey          , a   mid-wife       , on oath state that I attended on
Mrs.   Melissa Gibson       , wife of    Morris Gibson       on the   24th  day of

31

# Applications for Enrollment of Choctaw Newborn
## Act of 1905   Volume XX

November    , 1904; that there was born to her on said date a    female    child; that said child was living March 4, 1905, and is said to have been named  Motsy Gibson

her<br>
Agnes  x  Billey<br>
mark

Witnesses To Mark:
    { ABKimel    Antlers I.T.
    { Joe Wilson

    Subscribed and sworn to before me this  22$^{d}$  day of    June    , 1905

My commission expires Dec 1908        Eugene Easton
                            Notary Public.

-----

Choctaw 4130

Muskogee, Indian Territory, June 27, 1905.

Easton & Rowells,
    Attorneys at Law,
        Antlers, Indian Territory.

Gentlemen:

    Receipt is hereby acknowledged of your letter of June 22, transmitting affidavits of Melissa Gibson and Agnes Billey to the birth of Motsy Gibson, daughter of Morris and Melissa Gibson, November 24, 1904.

Respectfully,

Chairman.

-----

Choc New Born 1486
    Zachry[sic] T. Robinson
    (Born May 31, 1904)

-----

1486

## NEW BORN
### CHOCTAW
### ENROLLMENT

ZACHRY T. ROBINSON

(BORN MAY 31, 1904)

As Citizen of the
CHOCTAW NATION
Act of Congress
Approved March 3, 1905

C A N C E L L E D

RECORD TRANSFERRED TO CHOCTAW
NEW BORN #398

ACT OF CONGRESS APPROVED APRIL 26, 1906.

JULY 13, 1906

### 1486

---

## CHOCTAW   1486
## NEW BORN
ACT OF CONGRESS APPROVED MARCH 30, 1905.

*Zachry T. Robinson*
*(Born May 31, 1904)*

## CANCELLED
*Record transferred to*
*Choctaw New Born #398*
ACT OF CONGRESS APPROVED APRIL 26, 1906.

**JUL 13 1906**

Choc New Born 1487
  Thermon Davis
  (Born Aug 5, 1903)

1487

# NEW BORN
## CHOCTAW
### ENROLLMENT

THERMON DAVIS

(BORN AUGUST 5, 1903)

As Citizen of the
CHOCTAW NATION
Act of Congress
Approved March 3, 1905

TRANSFERRED TO 23-748
NOVEMBER 14, 1906.

**1487**

CHOCTAW     #1487
Act March 3 1905   NEW BORN

Thermon Davis
born Aug. 5, 1903

Transferred to 23-748
            Nov. 14, 1906.

Choc New Born 1488
>Sallie Coleman
>(Born Dec. 27, 1903)

*Jacket empty.*

---

1488

# NEW BORN
## CHOCTAW
### ENROLLMENT

SALLIE COLEMAN

(BORN DECEMBER 27, 1903)

As Citizen of the
CHOCTAW NATION
Act of Congress
Approved March 3, 1905

TRANSFERRED TO CHOCTAW
N.B.  (ACT OF APRIL 26, 1906) #177.

**1488**

---

Choc New Born 1489
>Jefferson Arnett
>(Born Nov. 29, 1904)

Cancelled

Record transferred to Choc.
New Born #534.

Act of Congress approved
Apr. 26, 1906.

July 13, 1906

---

1489

## NEW BORN
### CHOCTAW
ENROLLMENT

JEFFERSON ARNETT

(BORN NOVEMBER 29, 1904)


As Citizen of the
CHOCTAW NATION
Act of Congress
Approved March 3, 1905

RECORD TRANSFERRED TO CHOCTAW
NEW BORN # 534

ACT OF CONGRESS APPROVED APRIL 26, 1906.
JULY 13, 1906


1489

---

# CHOCTAW   1489

## NEW BORN
ACT OF CONGRESS APPROVED MARCH 30, 1905.

*Jefferson Arnett*
*(Born Nov. 29, 1904)*

# CANCELLED

*Record transferred to*
*Choctaw New Born #534*
ACT OF CONGRESS APPROVED APRIL 26, 1906.

**JUL 13 1906**

Choc New Born 1490
    Louise Dyer
    (Born Feb. 26, 1903)

----

**1490**

# NEW BORN

## CHOCTAW
### ENROLLMENT

### LOUISE DYER

(BORN FEBRUARY 26, 1903)

As Citizen of the
CHOCTAW NATION
Act of Congress
Approved March 3, 1905

REFUSED FEBRUARY 20, 1907
RECORD FORWARDED DEPARTMENT.  FEB. 20, 1907
ACTION APPROVED BY SECRETARY OF INTERIOR
            MARCH 4, 1907
NOTICE OF DEPARTMENTAL ACTION FORWARDED
ATTORNEYS FOR CHOCTAW AND CHICKASAW
NATIONS.  APRIL 3, 1907
NOTICE OF DEPARTANTAL[sic] ACTION FORWARDED
ATTORNEYS FOR APPLICANT.  APRIL 3, 1907
NOTICE OF DEPARTMENTAL ACTION MAILED
APPLICANT.  APRIL 3, 1907

**1490**

----

# Applications for Enrollment of Choctaw Newborn
## Act of 1905 Volume XX

## DEPARTMENT OF THE INTERIOR.
## COMMISSION TO THE FIVE CIVILIZED TRIBES.

---

IN RE APPLICATION FOR ENROLLMENT, as a citizen of the    Choctaw    Nation, of
Louise Dyer     , born on the  26"  day of  February  , 1903

Name of Father: Thomas D. Dyer        a citizen of the  Choctaw    Nation.
Name of Mother: Mary Dyer           a citizen of the  Choctaw    Nation.

Postoffice    Russellville, I. T.

---

### AFFIDAVIT OF MOTHER.

UNITED STATES OF AMERICA, Indian Territory, ⎱
   Western            DISTRICT. ⎰

    I,   Mary Dyer    , on oath state that I am................years of age and a citizen by
intermarriage   , of the   Choctaw   Nation; that I am the lawful wife of  Thomas D.
Dyer    , who is a citizen, by  intermarriage    of the    Choctaw    Nation; that
a   Female   child was born to me on   26th  day of  February    , 1903; that said
child has been named  Louise Dyer    , and was living March 4, 1905.

Mary Dyer

Witnesses To Mark:
  ⎰

    Subscribed and sworn to before me this  8th   day of   April     , 1905

Guy A. Curry
Notary Public.

(SEAL)

---

### AFFIDAVIT OF ATTENDING PHYSICIAN OR MID-WIFE.

UNITED STATES OF AMERICA, Indian Territory, ⎱
   Western            DISTRICT. ⎰

    I,   J. M. Turner     , a   physician     , on oath state that I attended on
Mrs.  Mary Dyer    , wife of  Thomas D. Dyer    on the 26th day of   February ,
1903; that there was born to her on said date a    Female    child; that said child was
living March 4, 1905, and is said to have been named Louise Dyer

J. M. Turner

Witnesses To Mark:

{

Subscribed and sworn to before me this  28th   day of   April        , 1905

Guy A. Curry
Notary Public.

(SEAL)

---

BIRTH AFFIDAVIT.

DEPARTMENT OF THE INTERIOR,
## COMMISSIONER TO THE FIVE CIVILIZED TRIBES.

ENROLLMENT OF MINORS.   ACT OF CONGRESS, APPROVED APRIL 26, 1906.

IN RE APPLICATION FOR ENROLLMENT, as a citizen of the        Choctaw        Nation,
of    Louise Dyer            , born on the    26th   day of   February   , 1903

Name of Father:  Thomas D. Dyer                  a citizen of the   Choctaw      Nation.
Name of Mother:  Mary Dyer                       a citizen of the   Choctaw      Nation.
                            Roll No.                                 Roll No.
Tribal enrollment of father intermarried /     Tribal enrollment of mother intermarried /

Postoffice        Quinton, I. T.

---

AFFIDAVIT OF MOTHER.

UNITED STATES OF AMERICA, Indian Territory, ⎫
   Western              District. ⎬

I,      Mary Dyer              , on oath state that I am   26      years of age
and a citizen by     intermarriage    , of the      Choctaw      Nation; that I am the
lawful wife of   Thomas D. Dyer    , who is a citizen, by     intermarriage      of the
Choctaw    Nation; that a   female   child was born to me on   26th   day of   February,
1903 , that said child has been named    Louise Dyer      , and was living March 4, 1906.

Mary Dyer

WITNESSES TO MARK:

{

Subscribed and sworn to before me this   18th   day of     May   , 1906.

Guy A. Curry
Notary Public.

(SEAL)

---

# Applications for Enrollment of Choctaw Newborn
# Act of 1905   Volume XX

AFFIDAVIT OF ATTENDING PHYSICIAN OR MID-WIFE.

UNITED STATES OF AMERICA, Indian Territory, ⎫
    Western                District. ⎭


I,    J. M. Turner          , a   physician       , on oath state that I attended on   Mrs. Mary Dyer   , wife of   Thomas D. Dyer   on the   26th  day of February  , 190 3; that there was born to her on said date a   female   child; that said child was living March 4, 1906, and is said to have been named   Louise Dyer

Dr. James M. Turner

WITNESSES TO MARK:
  ⎧ M. E. Trout
  ⎩ S. E. Willcox

Subscribed and sworn to before me this   16   day of     May   , 1906.

(SEAL)                         D. S. Willcox
My Commission Expires May 10th 1909.         Notary Public.

---

7-NB-1490.                                             O.L.J.

## DEPARTMENT OF THE INTERIOR,
## COMMISSIONER TO THE FIVE CIVILIZED TRIBES.

-----

In the matter of the application for the enrollment of Louise Dyer as a citizen by blood of the Choctaw Nation.

## D E C I S I O N.

It appears from the record herein that on April 29, 1905, application was made to the Commission to the Five Civilized Tribes for the enrollment of Louise Dyer as a citizen of the Choctaw Nation under the provisions of The Act of Congress approved March 3, 1905 (33 Stats., 1060). Subsequently, on May 19, 1906, application was made to the Commissioner to the Five Civilized Tribes for the enrollment of said applicant as a citizen of the Choctaw Nation under the provisions of The Act of Congress approved April 26, 1906 (34 Stats., 137).

It further appears from the record herein and the records in the possession of this office that the applicant, who is a white child, was born on February 26, 1903, and is the daughter of Thomas D. Dyer and Mary Dyer, whose names appear opposite numbers and , respectively, upon the final roll of citizens by blood of the Choctaw Nation, approved by the Secretary of the Interior; and that said applicant died   Nos. 1024 and 1023, respectively, upon the final roll of citizens by intermarriage of the Choctaw Nation approved by the Secretary of the Interior October 21, 1904.

I am, therefore, of the opinion that the application for the enrollment of Louise Dyer as a citizen of the Choctaw Nation should be denied, under the provisions of the Acts of Congress approved March 3, 1905 (33 Stats., 1060), and April 26, 1906 (34 Stats., 137), as amended by The Act of Congress approved June 21, 1906 (34 Stats., 325), and it is so ordered.

Tams Bixby   Commissioner.

Muskogee, Indian Territory.
FEB 20 1907

---

7-NB-1490

**COPY**

Muskogee, Indian Territory, February 20, 1907.

Thomas D. Dyer,
Russellville, Indian Territory.

Dear Sir:

Inclosed herewith you will find a copy of the decision of the Commissioner to the Five Civilized Tribes, rendered February 20, 1907, denying the application for the enrollment of Louise Dyer as a citizen of the Choctaw Nation.

The decision, with the record of proceedings in the case, is this day transmitted to the Secretary of the Interior for review. The final decision of the Secretary will be made known to you as soon as this office is informed of the same.

Respectfully,

SIGNED

*Tams Bixby*
Commissioner.

Registered.
Incl. 7NB-1490.

---

# Applications for Enrollment of Choctaw Newborn
## Act of 1905   Volume XX

7-NB-1490

Muskogee, Indian Territory, February 20, 1907.

McKennon & Dean,
    Attorneys-at-Law,
        South McAlester, Indian Territory.

Gentlemen:

Inclosed herewith you will find a copy of the decision of the Commissioner to the Five Civilized Tribes, rendered February 20, 1907, denying the application for the enrollment of Louise Dyer as a citizen of the Choctaw Nation.

The decision, with the record of proceedings in the case, is this day transmitted to the Secretary of the Interior for review. The final decision of the Secretary will be made known to you as soon as this office is informed of the same.

Respectfully,

SIGNED

*Tams Bixby*
Commissioner.

Registered.
Incl. 7-NB-1490.

---

7-NB-1490

Muskogee, Indian Territory, February 20, 1907.

Mansfield, McMurray & Cornish,
    Attorneys for Choctaw and Chickasaw Nations,
        South McAlester, Indian Territory.

Gentlemen:

Inclosed herewith you will find a copy of the decision of the Commissioner to the Five Civilized Tribes, rendered February 20, 1907, denying the application for the enrollment of Louise Dyer as a citizen of the Choctaw Nation.

The decision, with the record of proceedings in the case, is this day transmitted to the Secretary of the Interior for review. The final decision of the Secretary will be made known to you as soon as this office is informed of the same.

Respectfully,

SIGNED   *Tams Bixby*
Commissioner.

Incl. 7-NB-1490.

---

**COPY**

Muskogee, Indian Territory, February 20, 1907.

The Honorable,
The Secretary of the Interior.

Sir:

There is transmitted herewith record of the proceedings in the matter of the application for the enrollment of Louise Dyer as a citizen of the Choctaw Nation, including the decision of the Commissioner to the Five Civilized Tribes, dated February 20, 1907, denying said application.

Respectfully,

SIGNED   *Tams Bixby*
Commissioner.

2 Incl. 7-NB-1490.

Through the
Commissioner of Indian Affairs.

---

7-NB-1490.

Muskogee, Indian Territory, April 3, 1907.

Thomas D. Dyer,
Russellville, Indian Territory.

Dear Sir:

You are hereby advised that on March 4, 1907, the Secretary of the Interior affirmed the decision of this office of February 20, 1907, denying the application for the enrollment of Louise Dyer, as a citizen of the Choctaw Nation.

Respectfully,

*Geo. D. Rodgers.*
Acting Commissioner.

---

7-NB-1490.

Muskogee, Indian Territory, April 3, 1907.

McKennon & Dean,
    Attorneys-at-law,
        South McAlester, Indian Territory.

Gentlemen:

You are hereby advised that on March 4, 1907, the Secretary of the Interior affirmed the decision of this office of February 20, 1907, denying the application for the enrollment of Louise Dyer, as a citizen of the Choctaw Nation.

Respectfully,

*Geo. D. Rodgers.*
Acting Commissioner.

---

7-NB-1490.

Muskogee, Indian Territory, April 3, 1907.

Mansfield, McMurray & Cornish,
    Attorneys for Choctaw and Chickasaw Nations,
        South McAlester, Indian Territory.

Gentlemen:

You are hereby advised that on March 4, 1907, the Secretary of the Interior affirmed the decision of this office of February 20, 1907, denying the application for the enrollment of Louise Dyer, as a citizen of the Choctaw Nation.

Respectfully,

*Geo. D. Rodgers.*
Acting Commissioner.

---

F.P.

DEPARTMENT OF THE INTERIOR,

LRS.

WASHINGTON.                                    S.P.

March 4, 1907.

I.T.D.  6190, 7268, 7322, 7328, 7370-1907.
           7378, 7382-   "

D. C.  12855-1907.

DIRECT

Commissioner to the Five Civilized Tribes
        Muskogee, Indian Territory.

Sir:

Your decisions in the following Choctaw citizenship cases adverse to the applicants are hereby affirmed.  Copies of Indian Office letters submitting your report and recommending that the decisions be affirmed are inclosed.

|  | Date of your |
| Title of Cases. | letter of transmittal. |
| --- | --- |
| Eliza A. Alexander, et al. | February 15, 1907. |
| Nathan Brown      (freedman) | February   ?, 1907. |
| Louisa Dyer | February 20, 1907. |
| Mary Graham      (freedman) | February 20, 1907. |
| Hester S. Bailey | February 20, 1907. |
| Leroy Davis, et al.   (freedman) | February 11, 1907. |
| Nesbit Colbert      (freedman) | February   7, 1907. |

A copy hereof and the papers in the above mentioned cases have been sent to the Indian Office.

Respectfully,

E. A. Hitchcock

7 inc. and                                    Secretary.
14 to Ind. Of.

WCF 3/4/07.

---

Refer in reply to the following:
Land:  18954-1907.                                    Copy

DEPARTMENT OF THE INTERIOR,
OFFICE OF INDIAN AFFAIRS,
WASHINGTON, March 1, 1907.

The Honorable,
    The Secretary of the Interior.

Sir:

There is enclosed a report from Commissioner Bixby dated February 20, 1907, transmitting the record relative to the application for enrollment of Louise Dyer as a citizen of the Choctaw Nation. On February 20, 1907, the Commissioner held that the applicant was not entitled to enrollment.

The decision of the Commissioner has been examined and found to be correct, and its approval is recommended.

Very respectfully,

C.F.Larrabee,

Acting Commissioner.

JPB.GH.

------

7-4564.

Muskogee, Indian Territory, May 3, 1905.

Thomas D. Dyer,
    Russellville, Indian Territory.

Dear Sir:

Receipt is hereby acknowledged of the affidavits of Mary Dyer and J. M. Turner to the birth of Louise Dyer, daughter of Thomas D. and Mary Dyer, February 26, 1903, and the same have been filed with our records as an application for the enrollment of said child.

Respectfully,

Chairman.

------

7--4564.

Muskogee, Indian Territory, May 6, 1905.

Thomas D. Dyer,
    Russellville, Indian Territory.

Dear Sir:

Referring to the affidavits heretofore forwarded to the birth of Louise Dyer, daughter of Thomas Dyer and Mary Dyer, February 26, 1903.

You are advised that it appears from the affidavits and from our records that you and your wife, Mary Dyer, are both citizens by intermarriage of the Choctaw Nation. Under the provisions of The Act of Congress approved March 3, 1905, the Commission to the Five Civilized Tribes was authorized for a period of sixty days from that date to receive applications for the enrollment of children born to enrolled citizens by blood of the Choctaw and Chickasaw Nations.

You will therefore see that the Commission is without authority to enroll your child.

Respectfully,

Commissioner in Charge.

---

7-4546
7-NB-1490

Muskogee, Indian Territory, May 11, 1906.

T. D. Dyer,
    Quinton, Indian Territory.

Dear Sir:

Receipt is hereby acknowledged of your letter of May 4, 1906, inclosing affidavits of Mary Dyer and J. O. Briscoe to the birth of your child Rachel Dyer, December 19, 1905, and the same have been filed as an application for the enrollment of said child.

You also ask if it will be necessary for you to forward new application for the enrollment of your child Louise Dyer under the act of Congress approved April 26, 1906, and you are advised that you should forward new affidavits to the birth of your child Louise Dyer on the blank inclosed herewith.

# Applications for Enrollment of Choctaw Newborn
## Act of 1905    Volume XX

You are advised, however, that it appears from the records of this office that Louise and Rachel Dyer are the children to two intermarried citizens of the Choctaw Nation and under a recent opinion of the Assistant Attorney General white children of intermarried citizens of the Choctaw and Chickasaw Nations are not entitled to enrollment.

Respectfully,

B. C.                                                   Acting Commissioner.

---

7-2902
7-NB-1490
7-4665

Muskogee, Indian Territory, May 24, 1906.

Guy A. Curry,
    Quinton, Indian Territory.

Dear Sir:

Receipt is hereby acknowledged of your letter of May 18, 1906, transmitting the affidavits of John A. Sanders and A. C. Bullard M. D., to the birth of Monty Sanders, child of John A. and Mary Sanders, March 7, 1902; the affidavits of Mary Dyer and Dr. James M. Turner to the birth of Louise Dyer, child of Thomas D. and Mary Dyer, February 27, 1903, and the affidavits of Maybell King and Dr. D. S. Billington to the birth of Opal Louise King, child of Charles and Maybell King, October 26, 1905, and the same have been filed with the records of this office as applications for the enrollment of said children. the enrollment of the above named children.

Respectfully,

Acting Commissioner.

---

Choc New Born 1491
    Amaziah Milton
    (Born Feb. 5, 1904)

---

# Applications for Enrollment of Choctaw Newborn
## Act of 1905   Volume XX

### DEPARTMENT OF THE INTERIOR.
### COMMISSION TO THE FIVE CIVILIZED TRIBES.

---

IN RE APPLICATION FOR ENROLLMENT, as a citizen of the          Choctaw          Nation, of
Amaziah Melton          , born on the   5th   day of   February   , 1904

Name of Father:   George Melton          a citizen of the   Choctaw   Nation.
Name of Mother:   Betsy Melton          a citizen of the   Choctaw   Nation.

Postoffice   Muse I.T.

---

### AFFIDAVIT OF MOTHER.

UNITED STATES OF AMERICA, Indian Territory, ⎰
          Central          DISTRICT. ⎱

I,   Betsy Melton     , on oath state that I am   24     years of age and a citizen by
blood     , of the   Choctaw     Nation; that I am the lawful wife of   George Melton   ,
who is a citizen, by Blood   of the     Choctaw     Nation; that a     male     child
was born to me on   5th     day of     February 1904     , 1.........; that said child has been
named   Amaziah     , and was living March 4, 1905.

                                                    her
                                         Betsy   x   Melton
Witnesses To Mark:                              mark
⎰ Sidney Sage
⎱ M F Calhoun

Subscribed and sworn to before me this   22 day of     April     , 1905

My Com expires                              T. B. Lunsford
Feb. 4, 1908                                         Notary Public.

---

### AFFIDAVIT OF ATTENDING PHYSICIAN OR MID-WIFE.

UNITED STATES OF AMERICA, Indian Territory, ⎰
          Central          DISTRICT. ⎱

I,   Lazen Beams     , a   Mid-wife     , on oath state that I attended on
Mrs.   Betsy Melton     , wife of   George Melton     on the   5th   day of   February   ,
1904   1.......; that there was born to her on said date a     male     child; that said child
was living March 4, 1905, and is said to have been named   Amaziah

                                                    her
                                         Lazen   x   Beams
                                              mark

49

# Applications for Enrollment of Choctaw Newborn
## Act of 1905   Volume XX

Witnesses To Mark:
- Sidney Sage
- M F Calhoun

Subscribed and sworn to before me this   22   day of      April      , 1905

My Com expires                                    T. B. Lunsford
Feb. 4, 1908                                       Notary Public.

---

**BIRTH AFFIDAVIT.**

## DEPARTMENT OF THE INTERIOR.
## COMMISSION TO THE FIVE CIVILIZED TRIBES.

---

**IN RE APPLICATION FOR ENROLLMENT,** as a citizen of the        Choctaw        Nation, of
Amaziah Milton        , born on the   5" day of   February  , 1904

Name of Father:   George Milton              a citizen of the   Choctaw    Nation.
Name of Mother:   Bessie Milton *(Colbert)*    a citizen of the   Choctaw    Nation.
                                *Roll #5581*

Postoffice      Talihina  I.T.

---

**AFFIDAVIT OF MOTHER.**

UNITED STATES OF AMERICA, Indian Territory,
         Central            DISTRICT.

   I,   Bessie Milton  *(Colbert)*     , on oath state that I am   24     years of age and a
citizen by        blood      , of the      Choctaw      Nation; that I am the lawful wife of
George Milton   , who is a citizen, by  blood     of the        Choctaw        Nation; that a
male        child was born to me on   5"  day of      February       , 1904; that said child
has been named   Amaziah Milton      , and was living March 4, 1905.
                                                     her
                                            Bessie x Milton   *(Colbert)*
Witnesses To Mark:                                  mark
- C.E. Calhoun
- Sam T Roberts Jr

Subscribed and sworn to before me this   21st   day of      September       , 1905

My Com expires                                    T. B. Lunsford
Feb. 4, 1908                                       Notary Public.

---

# Applications for Enrollment of Choctaw Newborn
## Act of 1905   Volume XX

### AFFIDAVIT OF ATTENDING PHYSICIAN OR MID-WIFE.

UNITED STATES OF AMERICA, Indian Territory, ⎱
    Central            DISTRICT. ⎰

    I,    Lazen Beams      , a   midwife     , on oath state that I attended on Mrs.   Bessie Milton   , wife of    George Milton    on the 5" day of    February    , 1904; that there was born to her on said date a     male     child; that said child was living March 4, 1905, and is said to have been named   Amaziah Milton

her<br>
Lazen   x   Beams<br>
mark

Witnesses To Mark:
   ⎰ Joe Willie
   ⎱ G.W. Dukes

    Subscribed and sworn to before me this   21   day of      September    , 1905

My Com expires                     T. B. Lunsford
Feb. 4, 1908                             Notary Public.

---

## DEPARTMENT OF THE INTERIOR.
## COMMISSION TO THE FIVE CIVILIZED TRIBES.

    In the matter of the death of           Amaziah Milton
a citizen of the     Choctaw Nation      Nation, who formerly resided at or near     Talihina  ,
Ind. Ter., and died on the   9th   day of    September  , 1905

### AFFIDAVIT OF RELATIVE.

UNITED STATES OF AMERICA, Indian Territory, ⎱
    Central           DISTRICT. ⎰

    I,    George Milton     , on oath state that I am    22    years of age and a citizen by Blood  , of the   Choctaw   Nation; that my postoffice address is   Talihina     , Ind. Ter.; that I am     Father     of    Amaziah Milton      who was a citizen, by   Blood    , of the Choctaw    Nation and that said   Amaziah Milton    died on the   9th      day of   Sept  , 1905

George Milton

Witnesses To Mark:
   ⎰
   ⎱

51

# Applications for Enrollment of Choctaw Newborn
## Act of 1905   Volume XX

Subscribed and sworn to before me this   24th   day of   March   , 1906

W.A. Welch
Notary Public.

---

UNITED STATES OF AMERICA, Indian Territory, ⎫
Central                    DISTRICT.   ⎭

I,   Watson Potts   , on oath state that I am   28   years of age, and a citizen by Blood   of the Choctaw   Nation; that my postoffice address is   Talihina   , Ind. Ter.; that I was personally acquainted with   Amaziah Milton   who was a citizen, by   Blood , of the   Choctaw   Nation; and that said   Amaziah Milton   died on the   9th   day of September   , 1905

Watson Potts

Witnesses To Mark:

Subscribed and sworn to before me this   24th   day of   March   , 1906

W.A. Welch
Notary Public.

---

## LETTERS OF ADMINISTRATION.

UNITED STATES OF AMERICA,
INDIAN TERRITORY.
CENTRAL DISTRICT.
ANTLERS DIVISION. --SS

THE PRESIDENT OF THE UNITED STATES OF AMERICA,

TO ALL PERSONA[sic] TO WHOM THESE PRESENTS SHALL COME--GREETING:

KNOW YE, that whereas Amaziah Milton of the Central District of the Indian Territory, died intestate, as it is said, on or about the 9 day of Sept A.D., 1905, having at the time of his death personal property in the Indian Territory which may be lost, destroyed, or diminished in value, if speedy care be not taken of the same; to the end, therefore, that the said property may be collected preserved, and disposed of according to law, we do hereby appoint G. W. Dukes of said Central District of the Indian Territory, Administrator of all and singular the goods and chattels, rights and credits which were of the said Amaziah Milton at the time of his death, with full power and authority to dispose of the said property according to law, and to collect all moneys due the said deceased, and in general to do and perform all other acts and things which are or hereafter may be required of him by law.

Witness, the Honorable Thos C. Humphry, Judge of the United States Court in the Central District of the Indian Territory and the seal thereof, at Antlers in the Indian Territory, this 26 day of March A.D. 1906.

E. J. Fannin, Clerk,

( S E A L )                                                  By Jos R. Foltz, Deputy.

1729 - UNITED STATES COURT INDIAN TERRITORY CENTRAL DISTRICT. ADMINISTRATOR'S LETTERS. ESTATE OF Amaziah Milton, Deceased.

Recorded in Administrator's Record 3, Page 191, E. J. Fannin Clerk, By Jos R. Foltz, Deputy. Approved in open court Mar. 26-06. E. J. Fannin, Clerk, By Jos R. Foltz, D.C.

---

Helen A Smith, Stenographer to the Commissioner to the Five Civilized Tribes, on oath states that she copied the above letters of administration on the 31st day of March 1906, which is a full and true copy thereof.

Helen A Smith

Subscribed and sworn to before me this 31st day of March 1906.

H.C. Miller

N O T A R Y   P U B L I C.

---

Muskogee, Indian Territory, May 1, 1905.

George Melton,
   Muse, Indian Territory.

Dear Sir:

Receipt is hereby acknowledged of the affidavits of Betsy Melton and Lazen Beams to the birth of Amaziah Melton, son of George and Betsy Melton, February 5, 1904.

It is stated in the affidavits that you and Betsy Melton are both citizens by blood of the Choctaw Nation of the Choctaw Nation, and if this is correct you are requested to state the names under which you were enrolled, the names of your parents, and if you have selected allotments of the lands of the Choctaw and Chickasaw Nations please give your roll numbers as the same appear on the allotment certificates issued to yourself and your wife.

This matter should have immediate attention in order that proper disposition may be made of the application for the enrollment of the above named child.

Respectfully,

Chairman.

# Applications for Enrollment of Choctaw Newborn
## Act of 1905   Volume XX

Muskogee, Indian Territory, May 31, 1905.

George Melton,
Muse, Indian Territory.

Dear Sir:

Referring to the application for the enrollment of your child, Amaziah Melton, a letter was addressed to you on May 1, asking information which would enable us to identify the mother of this child upon our records.

Before further consideration can be given this application it will be necessary that you give the name under which your wife, Betsy Melton, was enrolled, her age, the names of her parents and other members of her family, and any other information which will enable the Commission to identify her upon its records.

This matter should receive immediate attention.

Respectfully,

Chairman.

Talihina, Ind Ter Aug 4th, 1905.

Hon Tams Bixby,
Commissioner to the Five Civilized Tribes,

Muskogee, Ind Ter.

My dear Sir:

Your letter of May 31st to me at Muse, Indian Territory I T has gone unanswered until today as I did not know what to do until I secured assistance. I notice you state "Before further consideration can be given this application it will be necessary that you give the name under which your wife, Bessie Melton was enrolled, her age, the names of her parents, and other members of her family &c."

You are advised that my wife's name prior to our marriage was "Bessie Colbert, a Choctaw by blood, enrollment number 5581 and her land was allotted on Jany 21st, 1905. in the Chickasaw Nation. Her fathers name was Johnson Colbert and her Mothers name was Salen Colbert. I thin, this was their names, however you can easily Locate her from her enrollment number. If you have any additional questions to complete the enrollment of our Son, Amaziah, I will thank you to address my Attorney, John J. Thomas, who will take care of the matter for me.

Yours truly,
George Melton.

———————

7-1948

Muskogee, Indian Territory, August 9, 1905.

George Melton,
   Talihina, Indian Territory.

Dear Sir:

Receipt is hereby acknowledged of your letter of August 4, 1905, stating that your wife was enrolled as Bessie Colbert a citizen by blood of the Choctaw Nation and that her roll number is 5581.

This information has enabled this office to identify your wife Bessie Colbert upon the approved roll of citizens by blood of the Choctaw Nation and the affidavits heretofore forwarded to the birth of your child Amaziah Melton have been filed as an application for the enrollment of said child.

Respectfully,

Acting Commissioner.

———————

7-NB-1491

Muskogee, Indian Territory, August 10, 1905.

George Melton,
   Talihina, Indian Territory.

Dear Sir:

In the matter of the enrollment of your child Amiziah[sic] Milton there are inclosed herewith partially filled out affidavits of Bessie Milton (Colbert) and Lazen Beams which you are requested to have reecuted[sic] and returned to this office as early as practicable.  Care should be taken to see that the name are signed as they appear in the body of the affidavits.

You are also requested to give the names of your parents and your roll number as it appears upon your allotment certificate.

It is believed that your name as it appears upon the approved roll of citizens by blood of the Choctaw Nation is Milton instead if Melton and if this is correct you are requested to have the affidavits herewith inclosed executed in the name of Milton as the same now appear.

Respectfully,

EB 1-10.                                                                Acting Commissioner.

---

7-NB-1491

Muskogee, Indian Territory, September 29, 1905.

John J. Thomas,
        Talihina, Indian Territory.

Dear Sir:

Receipt is hereby acknowledged of your letter of the 25th instant transmitting the affidavits of Bessie Milton and Lazen Beams relative to the birth of Amaziah Milton on February 5, 1904.

Said affidavits have been filed with the record in the matter of the application for the enrollment of said Amaziah Milton as a citizen by blood of the Choctaw Nation.

Respectfully,

Commissioner.

---

7-NB-1491

Muskogee, Indian Territory, November 9, 1905.

John J. Thomas,
        Talihina, Indian Territory.

Dear Sir:

Receipt is hereby acknowledged of your letter of November 6, 1905, asking the status of the application for the enrollment of Amaziah Melton, son of George and Bessie Melton.

In reply to your letter you are advised that the name of Amaziah Milton son of George and Bessie Milton has not yet been placed upon a schedule of new born citizens of the Choctaw Nation prepared for forwarding to the Secretary of the Interior, but his name will probably be placed upon the next schedule of such citizens prepared for that purpose.

Respectfully,

Commissioner.

Choc New Born 1492
>    Mary Elizabeth Terrell
>    (Born June 10, 1904)

---

**BIRTH AFFIDAVIT.**

## *DEPARTMENT OF THE INTERIOR.*
# COMMISSION TO THE FIVE CIVILIZED TRIBES.

---

*IN RE APPLICATION FOR ENROLLMENT,* as a citizen of the    Choctaw    Nation
of    Mary Elizabeth Terrell    , born on the    10$^{th}$    day of    June    , 1904

Name of Father: Elmer Terrell                a citizen of the    Choctaw    Nation.
Name of Mother: Louanna Smith Terrell        a citizen of the    Choctaw    Nation.

Postoffice    Chickasha I.T.

---

### *AFFIDAVIT OF MOTHER.*

UNITED STATES OF AMERICA, INDIAN TERRITORY, }
>    Southern          DISTRICT. 

I,   Louanna Smith Terrell    , on oath state that I am    about 33    years of age and a
citizen by    blood    , of the    Choctaw    Nation; that I am the lawful wife of    Elmer
Terrell    , who is a citizen, by    intermarriage    of the    Choctaw    Nation; that a
female    child was born to me on    10$^{th}$    day of    June    , 190 4, that said child has been
named    Mary Elizabeth Terrell    , and is now living.

Louanna Smith Terrell

WITNESSES TO MARK:

Subscribed and sworn to before me this   1$^{st}$   day of    April    , 1905.

Ado Melton
>    Notary Public.

---

57

# Applications for Enrollment of Choctaw Newborn
## Act of 1905   Volume XX

UNITED STATES OF AMERICA, INDIAN TERRITORY,
Southern                      DISTRICT.

I,    E. L. Dawson          , a   physician      , on oath state that I attended on
Mrs.  Louanna Smith Terrell    , wife of  Elmer Terrell    on the   10<sup>th</sup>   day of   June ,
190 4; that there was born to her on said date a      female      child; that said child is now living
and is said to have been named   Mary Elizabeth Terrell

E.L. Dawson, M.D.

WITNESSES TO MARK:

Subscribed and sworn to before me this  1<sup>st</sup>   day of    April        , 1905.

Ado Melton
Notary Public.

---

BIRTH AFFIDAVIT.

## DEPARTMENT OF THE INTERIOR.
## COMMISSION TO THE FIVE CIVILIZED TRIBES.

---

IN RE APPLICATION FOR ENROLLMENT, as a citizen of the        Choctaw       Nation, of
Mary Elizabeth Terrell      , born on the   10<sup>th</sup>   day of   June   , 1904

Name of Father: Elmer Terrell            a citizen of the   Choctaw    Nation.
Name of Mother: Louanna Smith Terrell         a citizen of the   Choctaw    Nation.

Postoffice     Chickasha Ind. Ter.

---

AFFIDAVIT OF MOTHER.

UNITED STATES OF AMERICA, Indian Territory,
Southern                      DISTRICT.

I,   Louanna Smith Terrell     , on oath state that I am    about 33    years of age
and a citizen by     Blood    , of the    Choctaw    Nation; that I am the lawful wife of
Elmer Terrell         , who is a citizen, by   intermarriage     of the      Choctaw
Nation; that a     female     child was born to me on   10<sup>th</sup>   day of   June    , 1904;
that said child has been named   Mary Elizabeth Terrell      , and was living March 4,
1905.

Louanna Smith Terrell

58

Witnesses To Mark:
{ T. Daniels
{ J.C. Terrell

Subscribed and sworn to before me this 4th   day of   April      , 1905

E. S. Burney
Notary Public.

---

**AFFIDAVIT OF ATTENDING PHYSICIAN OR MID-WIFE.**

UNITED STATES OF AMERICA, Indian Territory,
...................................................................DISTRICT. }

I,    E.L. Dawson          , a    physician        , on oath state that I attended on Mrs.  Louanna Smith Terrell          , wife of    Elmer Terrell      on the   10th   day of June      , 1904; that there was born to her on said date a      female      child; that said child was living March 4, 1905, and is said to have been named  Mary Elizabeth Terrell

E.L. Dawson, M.D.

Witnesses To Mark:
{ T. Daniels
{ J.C. Terrell

Subscribed and sworn to before me this 4th   day of   April      , 1905

E. S. Burney
Notary Public.

My time expires June 23rd 1906

---

Choctaw 434.

Muskogee, Indian Territory, April 8, 1905.

Bond & Melton,
    Attorneys at Law,
        Chickasha, Indian Territory.

Gentlemen:

Receipt is hereby acknowledged of your letter of April 2, enclosing the affidavits of Louanna Smith Terrell and E. L. Dawson to the birth of Mary Elizabeth Terrell, daughter of Eliner[sic] and Louanna Smith Terrell, June 10, 1904.

## Applications for Enrollment of Choctaw Newborn
## Act of 1905   Volume XX

You are advised that on October 15, 1904, the Commission to the Five Civilized Tribes refused the application of Louanna Smith Terrell for enrollment as a citizen by blood of the Choctaw Nation and the record in this case was, on October 31, 1904, transmitted to the Secretary of the Interior.

You are further advised that by an Act of Congress approved March 3, 1905, the Commission to the Five Civilized Tribes is only authorized to receive applications for the enrollment of children born to citizens by blood of the Choctaw and Chickasaw Nations whose enrollment had prior to that date been approved by the Secretary of the Interior.

You will therefore see that the Commission is without authority to enroll the child of Louanna Smith Terrell.

Respectfully,

Commissioner in Charge.

---

7-434

Muskogee, Indian Territory, April 11, 1905.

Elmer Terrell,
Chickasha, Indian Territory.

Dear Sir:

Receipt is hereby acknowledged of the affidavits of Louanna Smith Terrell and E. L. Dawson to the birth of Mary Elizabeth Terrell, daughter of Elmer and Louanna Smith Terrell, June 10, 1904.

It appears from our records that on October 15, 1904, the Commission to the Five Civilized Tribes rendered its decision refusing your application for enrollment as a citizen by blood of the Choctaw Nation and as The Act of Congress approved March 30[sic], 1905, only provides for the enrollment of children born to citizens by blood of the Choctaw and Chickasaw Nations whose enrollment had prior to that date been approved by the secretary of, you will therefore see that as you were advised in our previous letter the Commission is without authority to enroll your child.

Respectfully,

Commissioner in Charge.

Choc New Born 1493
 Joseph Allen Patterson
 (Born May 30, 1903)

**1493**

# NEW BORN
## CHOCTAW
### ENROLLMENT

JOSEPH ALLEN PATTERSON

(BORN MAY 30, 1903)

TRANSFERRED TO M.C.R.  N.B. #360

OCTOBER 23, 1906.

As Citizen of the
CHOCTAW NATION
Act of Congress
Approved March 3, 1905

**1493**

---

*(Act March (the remainder cut off corner)*
NEW BORN
*Joseph Allen Patterson*
*Born May 30 1903*

*Transferred to M. C. R.*
*N. B. #360*
*Oct. 23, 1906.*

Choc New Born 1494
>> Mary Jan Bohannon
>> *(Birthdate not given.)*

1494

# NEW BORN
## CHOCTAW
### ENROLLMENT

MARY JAN BOHANNON

As Citizen of the
## CHOCTAW NATION
Act of Congress
Approved March 3, 1905

TRANSFERRED TO 23-599

JANUARY 21, 1907.

## 1494

*1494*

*Choctaw* NEW BORN
*(Act March 3 1905)*

*Mary Jan Bohanon*[sic]

*Transferred to 23-599*
*Jan. 21 1907.*

Choc New Born 1495
  Aaron Homma
  (Born April 20, 1904)

1495

## NEW BORN
### CHOCTAW
### ENROLLMENT

AARON HOMMA

(BORN APRIL 20, 1904)

As Citizen of the
CHOCTAW NATION
Act of Congress
Approved March 3, 1905

CANCELLED

RECORD TRANSFERRED TO CHOCTAW
NEW BORN NO. 820.

ACT OF CONGRESS APPROVED APRIL 26, 1906.

**1495**

# CHOCTAW    1495
## NEW BORN
ACT OF CONGRESS APPROVED MARCH 30, 1905.

*Aaron Homma*
*(Born April 20, 1904)*

# CANCELLED
*Record transferred to*
CHOCTAW    NEW BORN *No 820*
ACT OF CONGRESS APPROVED APRIL 26, 1906.

# Applications for Enrollment of Choctaw Newborn
## Act of 1905   Volume XX

Choc New Born 1496
    Patsey Hickman
    (Born April 20, 1904)

_____

BIRTH AFFIDAVIT.

### DEPARTMENT OF THE INTERIOR.
### COMMISSION TO THE FIVE CIVILIZED TRIBES.

_____

IN RE APPLICATION FOR ENROLLMENT, as a citizen of the     Choctaw     Nation, of
Patsey Takubbe     , born on the  20$^{th}$  day of  April  , 1904

Name of Father: Jeff Takubbe         a citizen of the   Choctaw     Nation.
Name of Mother: Lizzie Takubbe         a citizen of the   Choctaw     Nation.

            Postoffice     Garvin, Ind. Ter.

_____

### AFFIDAVIT OF MOTHER.

UNITED STATES OF AMERICA, Indian Territory,⎤
    Central         DISTRICT.⎦

    I,   Lizzie Takubbe    , on oath state that I am  20  years of age and a citizen
by     Blood    , of the    Choctaw    Nation; that I am the lawful wife of   Jeff
Takubbe     , who is a citizen, by  Blood    of the     Choctaw     Nation; that a
Female    child was born to me on  20$^{th}$  day of    April    , 1904; that said child has
been named   Patsey Takubbe    , and was living March 4, 1905.

                  Lizzie Takubbe

Witnesses To Mark:
  ⎧
  ⎩

    Subscribed and sworn to before me this  First  day of    May    , 1905

                Simon Taylor
                Notary Public.

_____

### AFFIDAVIT OF ATTENDING PHYSICIAN OR MID-WIFE.

UNITED STATES OF AMERICA, Indian Territory,⎤
    Central         DISTRICT. ⎦

    I,   Louisa Wesley     , a   Midwife     , on oath state that I attended on
Mrs.   Lizzie Takubbe    , wife of   Jeff Takubbe    on the  20$^{th}$  day of   April    ,

1904; that there was born to her on said date a ............................ child; that said child was living March 4, 1905, and is said to have been named   Patsey Takubbe

her

Louisa  x  Wesley

mark

Witnesses To Mark:
  ⌠ Ephraim McKinney
  ⌡ Melvina Taylor

Subscribed and sworn to before me this  First   day of    May    , 1905

Simon Taylor
Notary Public.

---

*(The affidavit below typed as given.)*

DEPARTMENT OF THE INTERIOR, Commission to the Five Civilized Tribes:
IN RE  application for Enrollment of the Choctaw Nation.
of Patsy Takubbe.born on the 20th. day of April, 1904.

I, Lizzie Takubbe-nee Hickman, do solemnly swear that I am the Identical person who made application on or about the 2nd. day of May, 1905,for the enrollment of Patsy Takubbe as child of Lizzie Takubbe and Jeff Takubbe.

I further swear that   that part of said application which stated said child was the child of Jeff Takubbe, was an error.  It should have been Levi Takubbe,who is in fact the father of said child.

Lizzie Takubbe

Subscribed and sworn to before me.
this the 23rd. day of March, 1906.

T.G. Carr
Notary Public.

My Commission expires Sept 8, 1908.

---

## Applications for Enrollment of Choctaw Newborn
## Act of 1905    Volume XX

BIRTH AFFIDAVIT.

### DEPARTMENT OF THE INTERIOR.
## COMMISSION TO THE FIVE CIVILIZED TRIBES.

IN RE APPLICATION FOR ENROLLMENT, as a citizen of the          Choctaw          Nation, of
Patsey Tikubbi          , born on the   20th   day of   April   , 1904

Name of Father: Levi Tikubbi                    a citizen of the   Choctaw    Nation.
Name of Mother: Lizzie Tikubbi                  a citizen of the   Choctaw    Nation.

Postoffice

### AFFIDAVIT OF MOTHER.

UNITED STATES OF AMERICA, Indian Territory,
........................................................DISTRICT.

I,   Lizzie Tikubbi   , on oath state that I am   21    years of age and a citizen
by       blood      , of the      Choctaw      Nation; that I am the lawful wife of
........................................ , who is a citizen, by   blood      of the          Choctaw
Nation; that a     female      child was born to me on   20th     day of   April    , 1904;
that said child has been named    Patsey Tikubbi      , and was living March 4, 1905.

her
Lizzie x Tikubbi
Witnesses To Mark:                              mark
⎰ Elam M Ward
⎱ Cephus John

Subscribed and sworn to before me this 29th    day of      May      , 1906

*my com*
*Exp Mch 1909*              (Name Illegible)
Notary Public.

### AFFIDAVIT OF ATTENDING PHYSICIAN OR MID-WIFE.

UNITED STATES OF AMERICA, Indian Territory,
........................................................DISTRICT.

I,   Louisa Wesley      , a   midwife      , on oath state that I attended on
Mrs.   Lizzie Tikubbi      , wife of ......................................... on the   20th   day of
April    , 1904; that there was born to her on said date a    female    child; that said child
was living March 4, 1905, and is said to have been named   Patsey Tikubbi

her
Louisa x Wesley
mark

66

Witnesses To Mark:
- Elam M Ward
- Cephus John

Subscribed and sworn to before me this 29th   day of     May      , 1906

*my com*

*Exp Mch 1909*          *(Name Illegible)*

Notary Public.

---

**BIRTH AFFIDAVIT.**

### DEPARTMENT OF THE INTERIOR.
### COMMISSION TO THE FIVE CIVILIZED TRIBES.

---

**IN RE APPLICATION FOR ENROLLMENT,** as a citizen of the          Choctaw        Nation, of
Patsey  Hickman          , born on the   20    day of   April   , 1904

Name of Father: ................................................ a citizen of the ........................... Nation.
Name of Mother:  Lizzie Hickman              a citizen of the    Choctaw    Nation.

Postoffice      Garvin, I.T.

---

**AFFIDAVIT OF MOTHER.**

**UNITED STATES OF AMERICA, Indian Territory,**
   Western            **DISTRICT.**

I,    Lizzie Hickman    , on oath state that I am   22    years of age and a citizen
by        blood      , of the      Choctaw        Nation; ~~that I am the lawful wife of~~
~~——————————————, who is a citizen, by————————of the————————Nation;~~
that a     female    child was born to me on   20"    day of     April    , 1904; that said
child has been named    Patsey Hickman        , and was living March 4, 1905. *and that said*
*child died August 4, 1905*

Lizzie Hickman

Witnesses To Mark:

Subscribed and sworn to before me this  7  day of     August      , 1906

Walter W. Chappell
Notary Public.

---

67

7-NB-1496.

Department of the Interior,
Commissioner to the Five Civilized Tribes.
Muskogee, Indian Territory, August 7, 1906.

-----

In the matter of the application for the enrollment of Patsey Hickman as a citizen by blood of the Choctaw Nation.

LIZZIE HICKMAN, being first duly sworn, testified as follows:

Examination by the Commissioner:

Q What is your name? A Lizzie Hickman.
Q What is your age? A Twenty-two.
Q What is your father's name?  A I don't know.
Q What is your mother's name? A I don't know.
Q Have you any children? A I have two.
Q What are their names? A Julious Stevens.
Q What is the other one's name? A Patsey.
Q Is it Betsy or Patsey? A Patsey.
Q P-a-t-s-e-y is the way you spell it? A Yes.
Q You are now here in the matter of the application for the enrollment of this child, Patsey? A Yes.
Q Who is Patsey's father? A I don't know.
Q Then you desire to have this child enrolled under the name of Patsey Hickman?
A Yes.
Q Is Patsey Hickman living now? A No.
Q When did she die? A She died August 4, 1905.

It will be necessary for you to forward the affidavit of Louisa Wesley, the midwife who attended you at the birth of this child, as soon as you can, in order that disposition may be made of this application for enrollment.

(Witness excused.)

-----

Lenora B. Ashton, as stenographer to the Commissioner to the Five Civilized Tribes, on oath states that she reported the testimony in the above entitled cause on the 7th day of August, 1906, and that the above transcript is a true and complete translation of her stenographic notes.

Lenora B Ashton

Subscribed and sworn to before me this 8th day of August, 1906.

Walter W. Chappell
Notary Public.

-----

*7 nB 1496*

BIRTH AFFIDAVIT.

## DEPARTMENT OF THE INTERIOR.
## COMMISSION TO THE FIVE CIVILIZED TRIBES.

---

IN RE APPLICATION FOR ENROLLMENT, as a citizen of the        Choctaw        Nation, of
Patsey  Hickman        , born on the  20   day of  April  , 1904

~~Name of Father:~~ _____ ~~a citizen of the~~ ........................... Nation.
Name of Mother:  Lizzie Hickman        a citizen of the   Choctaw    Nation.

Postoffice      Garvin, I.T.

---

### AFFIDAVIT OF MOTHER.

UNITED STATES OF AMERICA, Indian Territory, ⎱
............................................................⎰DISTRICT.

I, ........................., on oath state that I am ..................years of age and a citizen by
........................, of the   ........................ Nation; that I am the lawful wife of
........................, who is a citizen, by ........................ of the ........................ Nation; that a
................ child was born to me on ..... day of ..............., 1......, that said child has been
named ........................................, and was living March 4, 1905.

Witnesses To Mark:
{ ........................................
........................................

Subscribed and sworn to before me this ....... day of ..............., 1905.

........................................
Notary Public.

---

### AFFIDAVIT OF ATTENDING PHYSICIAN OR MID-WIFE.

UNITED STATES OF AMERICA, Indian Territory, ⎱
     Central              DISTRICT. ⎰

I,   Louisa Wesley       , a   midwife       , on oath state that I attended on
Mrs.  Lizzie Hickman      , ~~wife of~~ _____ on the  20  day of  April   ,
1904; that there was born to her on said date a     female    child; that said child was
living March 4, 1905, and is said to have been named  Patsey Hickman
                                                    her
                                        Louisa  x  Wesley
                                                    mark

69

Witnesses To Mark:
- T.G. Carr
- *(Name Illegible)*

Subscribed and sworn to before me this 16<sup>th</sup> day of    August    , 1906

T.G. Carr
Notary Public.

My commission expires
Sept. 8, 1908

---

Muskogee, Indian Territory, May 6, 1905.

Lizzie Tabubbe,
  Garvin, Indian Territory.

Dear Madam:

Receipt is hereby acknowledged of your letter of May 1, 1905, enclosing affidavits of Lizzie Takubbe and Louisa Wesley to the birth of Patsey Takubbe, daughter of Jeff and Lizzie Takubbe, April 20, 1904.

It is stated in your affidavit that you are a citizen by blood of the Choctaw Nation. If this is correct you are requested to state the name under which you were enrolled, the names of your parents, and if you have selected an allotment of the lands of the Choctaw or Chickasaw Nations[sic] please give your roll number as it appears upon your allotment certificate.

Respectfully,

Commissioner in Charge.

---

Muskogee, Indian Territory, May 29, 1905.

Jeff Takubbe,
  Garvin, Indian Territory.

Dear Sir:

Referring to the application for the enrollment of your child, Patsey Takubbe, it is stated in the affidavits that you and your wife, Lizzie Takubbe, are citizens by blood of the Choctaw Nation, and if this is correct you are requested to state your ages, the names under which you were enrolled, the names of your parents, and if selection of allotments of the lands of the Choctaw or Chickasaw Nations[sic], have been made for you and your wife, give your roll numbers as the same appear upon your allotment certificates.

# Applications for Enrollment of Choctaw Newborn
## Act of 1905   Volume XX

This matter should receive immediate attention.

Respectfully,

Chairman.

---

Muskogee, Indian Territory, July 25, 1905.

Simon Taylor,
Garvin, Indian Territory.

Dear Sir:

Referring to the affidavits of Lizzie Takubbe and Louisa Wesley acknowledged before you May 1, 1905, to the birth of Patsey Takubbe, daughter of Jeff and Lizzie Takubbe, April 20, 1904, you are requested to state the name under which the mother of the child was enrolled, the names of her parents and if she has selected an allotment of the lands of the Choctaw or Chickasaw Nations[sic] please give her roll number as it appears upon her allotment certificate.

Respectfully,

Commissioner.

---

*(The letter below typed as given.)*

Garvin, I. T., August 18th, 1905.

Commission to the Five Civilized Tribes.
Muskogee, Ind. Ter.

Sir:

Your letter received sometime ago concerning Lizzie Takubbee wife of Jeff Takubbe,  In reply will say, the mother of Lizzie Hickman nee Takubbe was Emma Willis--The said Lizzie Hickman (nee Takubbe) was enrolled with her brother Coleman Hickman of Lukfata, Ind. Ter.  also please fine her (the said Lizzie Hickman (nee Takubbee's Roll number as it appears on her certificate of allotment--thus (No. 14617, Lizzie Hickman)  Hope this will be all satisfactorily information Concerning Lizzie Hickman for enrollment of her child Patsey Takubbe ect.

Hope to hear from your Commission after the action of Secretary of Interior for his approval

I remain

# Applications for Enrollment of Choctaw Newborn
## Act of 1905   Volume XX

Very Respectfully,

Simon Taylor,
for Lizzie Hickman (nee Talubbe)
Garvin, I.T.

———————

7-NB-1496

Muskogee, Indian Territory, November 3, 1905.

Lizzie Hickman,
    Care of Dennison & Latimer,
        Idabel, Indian Territory.

Dear Madam:

Receipt is hereby acknowledged of your letter of October 23, 1905, stating that you have received notice of the approval of your child Betsy Tokubee[sic] and you ask how long it will be before this child is approved.

In reply to your letter you are advised that May 2, 1905, there was received at this office affidavits of Lizzie Takubbe and Louisa Wesley to the birth of Patsy Takubbe, child of Jeff and Lizzie Takubbe, April 20, 1904.

Information was subsequently received which enabled this office to identify you upon its records as Lizzie Hickman, No. 14617 upon the approved roll of citizens by blood of the Choctaw Nation and the affidavits were filed as an application for the enrollment of your child.

You are further advised that this office is still unable to identify Jeff Takubbe upon its records as a citizen by blood of the Choctaw Nation. If you will state his age, the names of his parents, and his roll number, the matter of the enrollment of your child Patsy Takubbe will receive further consideration.

Respectfully,

Commissioner.

———————

7-NB-1496

Muskogee, Indian Territory, January 4, 1906.

Lizzie Takubbe,
        Care of Dennison & Latimer,
                Idabel, Indian Territory.

Dear Sir[sic]:

Referring to the application for the enrollment of your child Patsy Takubbe you are advised that it appears from the affidavits heretofore filed that Jeff Takubbe your husband, is a citizen by blood of the Choctaw Nation. This office is unable to identify him upon its records as an applicant for enrollment as a citizen of the Choctaw Nation and you are requested to state his full name, his age, the names of his parents, and if he has selected his allotment his roll number as it appears upon his allotment certificate. This matter should receive your immediate attention in order that disposition may be made of the application for the enrollment of your child Patsy Takubbe.

Respectfully,

Commissioner.

---

7-NB-1496

Muskogee, Indian Territory, March 15, 1906.

Lizzie Hickman,
        Care of T. M. Dumas,
                Madill, Indian Territory.

Dear Madam:

Receipt is hereby acknowledged of your letter of March 12, 1906, relative to an application made for the enrollment of Betsy[sic] Takubee, child of Levi Takubee and Lizzie Hickman born April 20, 1904; you state that affidavits were forwarded showing the birth of this child, but the mother did not remember whether said child was mentioned as Betsy Hickman or Betsy Takubee. You state, however, that neither the father nor mother has been notified of the enrollment of this child and you can find no trace of it having been enrolled under wither name and you ask the status of this case.

In reply to your letter you are advised that on May 2, 1905, there were received by the Commission to the Five Civilized Tribes affidavits of Lizzie Takubbe and Eliza Wesley to the birth of Patsy Takubbe, child of Jeff and Lizzie Takubbe, April 20, 1904.

# Applications for Enrollment of Choctaw Newborn
## Act of 1905   Volume XX

From the information contained in these affidavits this office was unable to identify either Jeff or Lizzie Takubbe upon its records as citizens of the Choctaw Nation, but on August 18, 1906, Lizzie Hickman advised this office that she was enrolled as a citizen by blood of the Choctaw Nation under the name of Lizzie Hickman opposite No. 14617 upon the approved roll of citizens by blood of said nation. No information has yet been received, however, which would identify Jeff Takubee[sic] as an applicant for enrollment.

In your letter it is noted you state the father of this child is named Levi Takubee and you are requested to advise the name under which he was enrolled and if he has selected an allotment of the lands of the Choctaw or Chickasaw Nation, his roll number as it appears upon his allotment certificate. Upon receipt of any information which will aid in identifying him upon its records the matter of the enrollment of Patsy Takubbe will receive further consideration.

Respectfully,

Acting Commissioner.

---

7-NB-1496

Muskogee, Indian Territory, May 18, 1906.

Elam M. Ward,
　　Glover, Indian Territory.

Dear Sir:

Receipt is hereby acknowledged of your letter of May 4, 1906, asking if Betsy Tekubee[sic] is approved; you state that the mother of this child is named Lizzie Hickman.

In reply to your letter you are advised that application has been made for the enrollment of Patsy Takubbe and from the record it appears that she is the child of Levi and Lizzie Takubbe. It appears, however that the citizen who is apparently the father of this child is enrolled as Tikubbi, and for the purpose of having the application for the enrollment of said child in proper form there is inclosed herewith a blank partially filled out which you are requested to have executed and returned to this office in the inclosed envelope.

Respectfully,

EB 1-18　　　　　　　　　　　　　　　　　　Acting Commissioner.
Env.

---

# Applications for Enrollment of Choctaw Newborn
## Act of 1905   Volume XX

7-NB-1496

Muskogee, Indian Territory, June 8, 1906.

E. M. Ward,
    Glover, Indian Territory.

Dear Sir:

Receipt is hereby acknowledged of your letter of May 29, 1906, inclosing affidavits of Lizzie Tikubbi and Louisa Wesley to the birth of Patsey Tikubbi, child of Levi an Lizzie Tikubbi, April 20, 1904, and the same have been filed with the record in this case.

Respectfully,

Commissioner.

_____

7-NB-1496
23-868

Muskogee, Indian Territory, November 24, 1906.

Elam M. Ward,
    Glover, Indian Territory.

Dear Sir:

Receipt is hereby acknowledged of your letter of November 16, 1906, asking if Listie Wilson and Patsy Tekabee have been approved.

In reply to your letter you are advised that the names of Listie Wilson and Patsy Hickman, children of Mercy Lewis and Lizzie Hickman have not yet been places upon a schedule of citizens of the Choctaw Nation prepared for forwarding to the Secretary of the Interior.

Respectfully,

Commissioner.

_____

7-NB-1496

Muskogee, Indian Territory, May 21, 1907.

T. M. Dumas,
    Madill, Indian Territory.

Dear Sir:

Receipt is hereby acknowledged of your letter of May 8, 1907, transmitting affidavit of Thompson Hickman to the death of Patsy Hickman a new born citizen of the Choctaw Nation which occurred September 6, 1905, and the same has been filed as evidence of the death of the above named child.

Respectfully,

Commissioner.

---

Choc New Born 1497
    Joseph James Wright
    (Born July 9, 1905)

**1497**

# NEW BORN
## CHOCTAW
### ENROLLMENT

JOSEPH JAMES WRIGHT

(BORN JULY 9, 1905)

As Citizen of the
CHOCTAW NATION
Act of Congress
Approved March 3, 1905

DECLINE TO RECEIVE OR CONSIDER NOVEMBER
16, 1905

## Applications for Enrollment of Choctaw Newborn
## Act of 1905   Volume XX

COPY OF DECISION FORWARDED ATTORNEYS FOR
CHOCTAW AND CHICKASAW NATIONS.  NOVEMBER
15, 1905
COPY OF DECISION FORWARDED APPLICANT
NOVEMBER 16, 1905
FORWARDED DEPARTMENT.  NOVEMBER 16, 1905
ACTION APPROVED BY SECRETARY OF INTERIOR
JANUARY 2, 1906
COPY OF DECISION FORWARDED ATTORNEYS FOR
CHOCTAW AND CHICKASAW NATIONS
JANUARY 22, 1906
NOTICE OF DEPARTMENTAL ACTION MAILED A[sic]
APPLICANT'S FATHER JANUARY 22, 1906
OCTOBER 31, 1906  DEPARTMENT REQUESTED TO RE-
TURN RECORD FOR READJUDICATION UNDER ACT
OF APRIL 26, 1906   NOVEMBER 24, 1906  DEPT.

ACTION OF *JUNE 2 1906*

RESCINDED AND CASE RETURNED FOR READJUDICATION.


### 1497

---

DEPARTMENT OF THE INTERIOR,
COMMISSIONER TO THE FIVE CIVILIZED TRIBES.

Record in the matter of the application for enrollment as a citizen by blood of the Choctaw Nation of - -

Joseph James Wright.

7-NB-1497.

---

BIRTH AFFIDAVIT.

# DEPARTMENT OF THE INTERIOR,
### COMMISSION TO THE FIVE CIVILIZED TRIBES.

---

*IN RE Application for Enrollment,* as a citizen of the        Choctaw        Nation,
of   Joseph James Wright  , born on the  9"    day of   July   , 1905

| Name of Father: | E B Wright | a citizen of the  Choctaw | Nation. |
| Name of Mother: | Francis Wright | a citizen of the  Choctaw | Nation. |

Post-Office:        Stuart IT

# Applications for Enrollment of Choctaw Newborn
## Act of 1905   Volume XX

---

### AFFIDAVIT OF MOTHER.

---

UNITED STATES OF AMERICA,
**INDIAN TERRITORY.**
Central                 District.

I,     Francis Wright          , on oath state that I am   25    years of age and a citizen by     Birth     , of the  Choctaw   Nation; that I am the lawful wife of   E B Wright    , who is a citizen, by     Birth     of the  Choctaw   Nation; that a      male     child was born to me on    9" day of    July   , 190 5, that said child has been named    Joseph James Wright   , and is now living.

her

Francis x Wright

mark

**WITNESSES TO MARK:**

{ Elias Wesley
{ Carney Ott

*Subscribed and sworn to before me this*   24"  *day of*    Aug      , *1905.*

My com exp July 8 1908                              J H Elliott

*NOTARY PUBLIC.*

---

### AFFIDAVIT OF ATTENDING PHYSICIAN OR MID-WIFE.

---

UNITED STATES OF AMERICA,
**INDIAN TERRITORY.**
Central                 District.

I,     Eliza Ott         , a    midwife           , on oath state that I attended on Mrs.  Wright    , wife of   EB Wright     on the    9"    day of     July   , 1905 ; that there was born to her on said date a      male     child; that said child is now living and is said to have been named     Joseph James Wright

her

Eliza x Ott

mark

**WITNESSES TO MARK:**

{ Elias Wesley
{ Carney Ott

*Subscribed and sworn to before me this*   23  *day of*    Aug      , *1905.*

J H Elliott

*NOTARY PUBLIC.*

My com exp July 8 1908

---

78

# Applications for Enrollment of Choctaw Newborn
## Act of 1905   Volume XX

7-NB-1497.

DEPARTMENT OF THE INTERIOR,
COMMISSIONER TO THE FIVE CIVILIZED TRIBES.

In the matter of the application for the enrollment of Joseph James Wright as a citizen by blood of the Choctaw Nation.

- - : D E C I S I O N : - -

It appears from the record in this case that on August 26, 1905, there was filed with the Commissioner to the Five Civilized Tribes an application for the enrollment of Joseph James Wright as a citizen by blood of the Choctaw Nation.

It further appears from the record herein, and the records of the Commission to the Five Civilized Tribes, that the applicant was born July 9, 1905, and is a son of E. B. Wright, a recognized and enrolled citizen by blood of the Choctaw Nation whose name (as Eslam Wright) appears as No. 12859 upon the final roll of citizens by blood of the Choctaw Nation approved by the Secretary of the Interior March 6, 1903, and Frances Wright, a recognized and enrolled citizen by blood of the Choctaw Nation who name appears as No. 120 upon the final roll of citizens by blood of the Choctaw Nation approved by the Secretary of the Interior December 12, 1902.

The Act of Congress approved March 3, 1905 (Public No. 212) among other things provides:

"That the Commission to the Five Civilized Tribes is authorized for sixty days after the date of the approval of this act to receive and consider applications for enrollment of children born subsequent to September twenty-fifth, nineteen hundred and two, and prior to March fourth, nineteen hundred and five, and who were living on said latter date, to citizens by blood of the Choctaw and Chickasaw tribes of Indians whose enrollment has been approved by the Secretary of the Interior prior to the date of the approval of this act; and to enroll and make allotments to such children."

I am of the opinion that, inasmuch as said Joseph James Wright was not born prior to March 4, 1905, and no application having been made for his enrollment within the time limited by the provisions of law above quoted, I am without authority to receive or consider the application for his enrollment as a citizen by blood of the Choctaw Nation, and that therefore, I should decline to receive or consider such application, and it is so ordered.

Tams Bixby      Commissioner.

Muskogee, Indian Territory.
NOV 16 1905

7-NB-1497                                                   **COPY**

Muskogee, Indian Territory, November 16, 1905.

E. B. Wright,
Stuart, Indian Territory.

Dear Sir:

Inclosed herewith you will find a copy of the decision of the Commissioner to the Five Civilized Tribes, rendered November 16, 1905, declining to receive or consider the application for the enrollment of your infant child, Joseph James Wright, as a citizen by blood of the Choctaw Nation.

The decision, with the record of proceedings in the case, is this day transmitted to the Secretary of the Interior for review. The final decision of the Secretary will be made known to you as soon as this office is informed of the same.

Respectfully,

SIGNED   *Tams Bixby*
Registered.                                              Commissioner
Incl. 7-NB-1497

---

7-NB-1497                                                   **COPY**

Muskogee, Indian Territory, November 16, 1905.

Mansfield, McMurray & Cornish,
Attorneys for Choctaw and Chickasaw Nations,
South McAlester, Indian Territory.
Gentlemen:

Inclosed herewith you will find a copy of the decision of the Commissioner to the Five Civilized Tribes, rendered November 16, 1905, declining to receive the application for the enrollment of Joseph James Wright as a citizen by blood of the Choctaw Nation.

The decision, with the record of proceedings in the case, is this day transmitted to the Secretary of the Interior for review. The final decision of the Secretary will be made known to you as soon as this office is informed of the same.

Respectfully,

SIGNED   *Tams Bixby*
Commissioner

Incl. 7-NB-1497

---

Refer in reply                                                                                                COPY.
  to the
following:

DEPARTMENT OF THE INTERIOR,

LAND:
92816-1905.                        OFFICE OF INDIAN AFFAIRS,

WASHINGTON.

December 22, 1905.

The Honorable,
    The Secretary of the Interior.

Sir:

    I have the honor to enclose a report from the Commissioner to the Five Civilized
Tribes, dated November 16, 1905, transmitting the record of the application made August
26, 1905, for enrollment as a citizen by blood of the Choctaw Nation, of Joseph James
Wright, November 16, 1905, the Commissioner decided adversely to the applicant.

    The record shows that no prior application has been made and that the applicant
was born July 9, 1905.

    In view of the record and of the Act of March 3, 1905 (33 Stats., 1060), the
approval of the Commissioner's decision adverse to the applicatn[sic] is recommended.

Very respectfully,

C. F. Larrabee,

Acting Commissioner.

M.M.M. - NL.

---

J.P.

COPY

DEPARTMENT OF THE INTERIOR,

FHE.

WASHINGTON.

D. C.        803-1906.                                    January 2, 1906.
I.TD.       17896-1905.

L.R.S.

Commissioner to the Five Civilized Tribes,
    Muskogee, Indian Territory.

Sir:

November 16, 1905, you transmitted the record in the matter of the application for the enrollment of Joseph James Wright as a citizen by blood of the Choctaw Nation, including your decision of the same date, declining to receive said application.

Reporting December 22, 1905, the Indian Office recommends that said decision be approved. A copy of its letter is inclosed.

The Department concurs in said recommendation, and your decision is hereby affirmed.

Respectfully,

(Signed) Thos. Ryan,
First Assistant Secretary.

1 inclosure.

———————

7-NB-1497.

Muskogee, Indian Territory, January 22, 1906.

E. B. Wright,
    Stuart, Indian Territory.

Dear Sir:

You are hereby advised that on January 2, 1906, the Secretary of the Interior affirmed the decision of the Commissioner to the Five Civilized Tribes of November 16, 1905, declining to receive or consider the application for the enrollment of your infant child, Joseph James Wright, as a citizen by blood of the Choctaw Nation.

Respectfully,

Commissioner.

---

7-NB-1497.

Muskogee, Indian Territory, January 22, 1906.

Mansfield, McMurray & Cornish,
    Attorneys for Choctaw and Chickasaw Nations,
        South McAlester, Indian Territory.

Gentlemen:

You are hereby advised that on January 2, 1906, the Secretary of the Interior affirmed the decision of the Commissioner to the Five Civilized Tribes of November 16, 1905, declining to receive or consider the application for the enrollment of your infant child, Joseph James Wright, as a citizen by blood of the Choctaw Nation.

Respectfully,

Commissioner.

---

Muskogee, Indian Territory, October 31, 1906.

The Honorable,
    The Secretary of the Interior.

Sir:

November 16, 1905, the Commissioner to the Five Civilized Tribes rendered a decision declining to receive or consider the application for the enrollment of Joseph James Wright as a citizen of the Choctaw Nation under the Act of Congress approved March 3, 1905 for the reason that said child was born subsequent to March 3, 1905, and on January 2, 1906 (I.T.D. 17896-1905) this action was approved by the Secretary of the Interior.

In view of the provision of Section 2 of The Act of Congress approved April 26, 1906, I have the honor to request that the record in this case be returned for readjudication under said act.

Respectfully,

Through the Commissioner                              Commissioner.
    of Indian Affairs.

---

DEPARTMENT OF THE INTERIOR,                    J.P.

WASHINGTON.                          FHE.

I.TD.    23268-1906.                              November 24, 1906.
D. C.  52125

L.R.S.

Commissioner to the Five Civilized Tribes,
   Muskogee, Indian Territory.

Sir:

In accordance with the recommendation contained in your letter of October 31, 1906, and in view of the provisions of section 2 of the act of April 26, 1906 (34 Stat., 137), the record in the Choctaw enrolment[sic] case of Joseph J. Wright is inclosed for readjudication. This applicant was born subsequent to March 3, 1905.

The decision of the Department of January 2, 1906, affirming your decision adverse to the claimant, is rescinded.

A copy of Indian Office letter of November 20, 1906 (Land 96981), submitting your report, is inclosed.

Respectfully,

Thos Ryan

Through the Commissioner                    First Assistant Secretary.
   of Indian affairs.

2 inclosures.

---

---COPY--

DEPARTMENT OF THE INTERIOR,
Land                OFFICE OF INDIAN AFFAIRS
WASHINGTON.
754-1906.
96981-1906.                          November 20, 1906.

The Honorable,
   The Secretary of the Interior.

Sir:

Referring to Departmental letter of January 2, 1906 (I.T.D. 17896-1905), affirming the decision of the Commissioner to the Five Civilized Tribes, rejecting the application of Joseph James Wright for enrollment as a citizen by blood of the Choctaw Nation, I have the honor to transmit herewith a communication from the Commissioner, dated October 31, 1906, requesting that the record in this case be returned to him for readjudication under section 2 of The Act of Congress approved April 26, 1906, (34 Stat. 137).

The record in the case is also transmitted.

Very respectfully,

C. F. Larrabee,

Acting Commissioner.

EWE-EH

---

7-NB-1497

Muskogee, Indian Territory, August 26, 1905.

E. B. Wright,
Stuart, Indian Territory.

Dear Sir:

Receipt is hereby acknowledged of the affidavits of Francis Wright and Eliza Ott to the birth of Joseph James Wright, child of E. B. and Francis Wright, July 9, 1905.

You are advised that under the provisions of the act of Congress approved March 3, 1905, there is no provisions for the enrollment of children born to enrolled citizens by blood of the Choctaw and Chickasaw Nation[sic], subsequent to March 3, 1905.

Respectfully,

Commissioner.

---

## Applications for Enrollment of Choctaw Newborn
## Act of 1905   Volume XX

Muskogee, Indian Territory, January 25, 1906.

Chief Clerk,
Choctaw Land Office,
Atoka, Indian Territory.

Dear Sir:

There are inclosed herewith copies of Choctaw New Born cards as follows:

No. 1497, Joseph James Wright.
No. 1500, Eliza Jane Jennings.

These cards were not in the files when the Choctaw and Chickasaw roll cards were forwarded you on yesterday, for the purpose of making the records of your office conform to those of the General Office.

Respectfully,

Acting Commissioner.

LBA 3/25.

----

Muskogee, Indian Territory, January 25, 1906.

Chief Clerk,
Chickasaw Land Office,
Ardmore, Indian Territory.

Dear Sir:

There are inclosed herewith copies of Choctaw New Born cards as follows:

No. 1497, Joseph James Wright.
No. 1500, Eliza Jane Jennings.

These cards were not in the files when the Choctaw and Chickasaw roll cards were forwarded you on yesterday, for the purpose of making the records of your office conform to those of the General Office.

Respectfully,

Acting Commissioner.

LBA 4/25.

Choc. New Born 1498
*(Amison Mullen)*
*(Born January 15, 1905)*

---

**BIRTH AFFIDAVIT.**

## DEPARTMENT OF THE INTERIOR.
## COMMISSION TO THE FIVE CIVILIZED TRIBES.

---

**IN RE APPLICATION FOR ENROLLMENT,** as a citizen of the Choctaw Nation, of
Amison Mullen , born on the 15$^{th}$ day of January , 1905

Name of Father: Morris Mullen          a citizen of the  Choctaw  Nation.
Name of Mother:  Winy Mullen          a citizen of the  Choctaw  Nation.

Postoffice    Higgins, Indian Territory

---

**AFFIDAVIT OF MOTHER.**

UNITED STATES OF AMERICA, Indian Territory, ⎫
       Central                DISTRICT. ⎭

I,   Winy Mullen   , on oath state that I am   Thirty   years of age and a citizen by   blood   , of the   Choctaw   Nation; that I am the lawful wife of   Morris Mullen   , who is a citizen, by blood   of the   Choctaw   Nation; that a male   child was born to me on   15$^{th}$   day of   January   , 1905; that said child has been named   Amison Mullen   , and was living March 4, 1905.

                                            her
                              Winy  x  Mullen
Witnesses To Mark:                          mark
  ⎰ Stephen Cooper
  ⎱ Wilcox Bee

Subscribed and sworn to before me this 1$^{st}$ day of  April  , 1905

                          Wm J Hulsey
                                Notary Public.

---

87

# Applications for Enrollment of Choctaw Newborn
## Act of 1905   Volume XX

### AFFIDAVIT OF ATTENDING PHYSICIAN OR MID-WIFE.

UNITED STATES OF AMERICA, Indian Territory,
Central            DISTRICT.

I,   Morris Mullen         , a   attendant        , on oath state that I attended on Mrs.   Winy Mullen       , wife of   myself      on the   15<sup>th</sup>   day of   January   , 1905; that there was born to her on said date a   male   child; that said child was living March 4, 1905, and is ~~said to have been~~ named   Amison Mullen   *That we were unable to secure a physician or midwife*

Morris Mullen

Witnesses To Mark:

{

Subscribed and sworn to before me this 1<sup>st</sup>   day of   April   , 1905

Wm J Hulsey<br>Notary Public.

---

*(The affidavit below typed as given.)*

*Hartshorne Ind Ter*                    *September 16/1905*
*Affidavit*

*I Wilburn Taylor after being sworn deposes and states that his name is Wilburn Taylor that his post office address is Higgins Ind Ter That he is acquainted with Morris Mullen and his wife Winey Mullen and there child Amison Mullen. That I was at Morris Mullen about three days after the birth of the child Amison Mullen. Whitch was about January the 15/1908. And I futher state that the said child was living on March the 4 1905 - and is living at present and I futher state that I have no interest in said claim and I am not related to any of said partys.*

*Wilburn Taylor*

*Subscribed and sworn to before me this sworn to before me a Notary Public for the Central District Indian Territory this the 16 day of September 1905*

My COmmission Expires
MAY 20 1908 ;
*Samuel A Maysey Notary Public*

---

# Applications for Enrollment of Choctaw Newborn
## Act of 1905   Volume XX

*(The affidavit below typed as given.)*

*Hartshorne Ind Ter*                    *September the 16/1905*

*Affidavit*

*John Pulcher after being duly sworn deposes and says that he is the Judge of Gaine County Choctaw Nation and that he is acquainted with Morris Mullen and his wife Winey Mullen and the child Amison Mullen   That he married Morris Mullen to his present wife who was at the time of marriage the Widow Reed and known as Winey Reed that he saw the child Amison Mullen soon after its birth that said child was living the 4 day of March 1905 - and that he has no interest in said (illegible) and is not related to any of the partyes herein named*

*That his Post office is Hartshorne Ind Ter*

*John Pulcher*

*Subscribed and sworn to before me a Notary Public for the Central District Indian Territory this the 16 day of September 1905*

My COmmission Expires
MAY 20 1908 ;

*Samuel A Maysey Notary Public*

---

Choctaw 3126.

Muskogee, Indian Territory, April 7, 1905.

Morris Mullen,
    Higgins, Indian Territory.

Dear Sir:

Receipt is hereby acknowledged of the affidavits of Winy Mullen and Morris Mullen to the birth of Amison Mullen, son of Morris and Winy Mullen, January 15, 1905.

It is stated in the affidavit of the mother that she is a citizen by blood of the Choctaw Nation. It this is correct, you are requested to state when, where and under what name she was enrolled, the names of her parents and any other information you may possess which will enable us to identify her upon our records.

This matter should receive immediate attention in order that disposition may be made of the application for the enrollment of the child herein named.

# Applications for Enrollment of Choctaw Newborn
## Act of 1905   Volume XX

Respectfully,

Commissioner in Charge.

---

Muskogee, Indian Territory, May 31, 1905.

Morris Mullen,
    Higgins, Indian Territory.

Dear Sir:

Referring to the application for the enrollment of your child, Amison Mullen, a letter was addressed to you on April 7, 1905, asking information which would enable us to identify the mother of this child.

Before further consideration can be given this application it will be necessary that you give the name under which your wife, Winy Mullen, was enrolled, her age, the names of her parents and other members of her family, and any other information which will enable the Commission to identify her upon our records.

This matter should receive immediate attention.

Respectfully,

[sic]

---

Hartshorne, Indian Territory, August 28, 1905.

Hon Tams Bixby,
    Muskogee, I. T.

Sir:

Please inclosed letter of yours Dated May 31/1905 which will explain this note. Amison Mullen mother was enrolled as Winey Reed. Her father name was John Carr. Mother named Eliza Carr. Brothers name Osbon Carr Dennis Carr.

Resp

Morris Mullen.

---

7-NB-1498.

Muskogee, Indian Territory, August 31, 1905.

Morris Mullen,
    Hartshorne, Indian Territory.

Dear Sir:

Receipt is hereby acknowledged of your letter, without date, received at this office the 29th instant, giving information relative to the enrollment as a citizen by blood of the Choctaw Nation of your wife, Winey Mullen, in the matter of the application for the enrollment of your infant child, Amison Mullen.

You are advised that the information contained in your letter has enabled this office to identify your wife upon the records as a citizen by blood of the Choctaw Nation.

You are further advised that it appears, from the affidavits heretofore filed in the matter of the enrollment of your said child, Amison Mullen, that you were the only one in attendance upon your wife at the birth of said child, in this event it will be necessary that you furnish the affidavits of two disinterested witnesses who are not related to the applicant and have actual knowledge of the facts that the child was born, the date of its birth; that it was living on march[sic] 4, 1905, and that Winey Mullen is its mother.

You should give this matter immediate attention, as no further action can be taken, relative to the enrollment of said child, until this information is furnished.

Respectfully,

Commissioner.

---

7-NB-1498

Muskogee, Indian Territory, September 22, 1905.

Morris Mullin,
    Higgins, Indian Territory.

Dear Sir:

Receipt is hereby acknowledged of the affidavits of Wilburn Taylor and John Pulcher, relative to the birth of your minor son Amison Mullin, and said affidavits have been filed with the record in the matter of the application for the enrollment of the said Amison Mullin as a citizen by blood of the Choctaw Nation.

# Applications for Enrollment of Choctaw Newborn
## Act of 1905   Volume XX

Respectfully,

Acting Commissioner.

---

7-NB-1498

Muskogee, Indian Territory, February 10, 1906.

Morris Mullin,
Higgins, Indian Territory.

Dear Sir:

Receipt is hereby acknowledged of your letter of February 7, 1906, asking if your minor child Amison Mullin has been enrolled and is entitled to an allotment.

In reply to your letter you are advised that the name of your child Amison Mullin has been placed upon a schedule of new born citizens of the Choctaw Nation which has been forwarded the Secretary of the Interior and you will be notified when his enrollment is approved by the Department.

Respectfully,

Acting Commissioner.

---

Choc. New Born 1499
Ruth Frazier
(Born Dec. 27, 1903)

---

BIRTH AFFIDAVIT.

## DEPARTMENT OF THE INTERIOR.
## COMMISSION TO THE FIVE CIVILIZED TRIBES.

---

IN RE APPLICATION FOR ENROLLMENT, as a citizen of the            Choctaw        Nation, of
Ruth Frazier          , born on the 27   day of  December   , 1903

Name of Father:  Hudson Frazier                    a citizen of the   Choctaw     Nation.
Name of Mother:  Miriam Frazier                    a citizen of the   Choctaw     Nation.

Postoffice      Duncan, Indian Territory

---

92

# Applications for Enrollment of Choctaw Newborn
## Act of 1905   Volume XX

### AFFIDAVIT OF MOTHER.

UNITED STATES OF AMERICA, Indian Territory, ⎱
    Southern           DISTRICT. ⎰

I,     Miriam Frazier   , on oath state that I am   25    years of age and a citizen by     blood   , of the     Choctaw     Nation; that I am the lawful wife of    Hudson Frazier    , who is a citizen, by   blood     of the      Choctaw      Nation; that a female     child was born to me on   27th   day of   December,    , 1905[sic]; that said child has been named    Ruth Frazier    , and was living March 4, 1905.

Miriam Frazier

Witnesses To Mark:

     { 

        Subscribed and sworn to before me this   6th   day of     April      , 1905

Edna Bowerman<br>Notary Public.

---

### AFFIDAVIT OF ATTENDING PHYSICIAN OR MID-WIFE.

UNITED STATES OF AMERICA, Indian Territory, ⎱
    Southern           DISTRICT. ⎰

I,     J.L. Wharton      , a     physician     , on oath state that I attended on Mrs.    Miriam Frazier      , wife of     Hudson Frazier     on the    27   day of December,    , 1905[sic]; that there was born to her on said date a     female      child; that said child was living March 4, 1905, and is said to have been named    Ruth Frazier

J.L. Wharton

Witnesses To Mark:

     {

        Subscribed and sworn to before me this   6th   day of    April      , 1905

Edna Bowerman<br>Notary Public.

---

# Applications for Enrollment of Choctaw Newborn
## Act of 1905   Volume XX

BIRTH AFFIDAVIT.
## DEPARTMENT OF THE INTERIOR.
## COMMISSION TO THE FIVE CIVILIZED TRIBES.

---

IN RE APPLICATION FOR ENROLLMENT, as a citizen of the      Choctaw      Nation, of
Ruth Frazier      , born on the 27<sup>th</sup>   day of   December   , 1903

Name of Father: Hudson Frazier                    a citizen of the   Choctaw   Nation.
Name of Mother:  Marion Frazier                    a citizen of the   Choctaw   Nation.

Postoffice      Arthur Ind Ter

---

### AFFIDAVIT OF MOTHER.

UNITED STATES OF AMERICA, Indian Territory, ⎫
      Southern            DISTRICT. ⎭

I,    Marion Frazier    , on oath state that I am   25    years of age and a citizen
by      blood    , of the    Choctaw    Nation; that I am the lawful wife of    Hudson
Frazier          , who is a citizen, by   blood    of the        Choctaw      Nation; that a
female      child was born to me on   27<sup>th</sup>   day of   December      , 1903; that said
child has been named   Ruth Frazier      , and was living March 4, 1905.

Marion Frazier

Witnesses To Mark:
⎰

Subscribed and sworn to before me this   4<sup>th</sup>   day of      September      , 1905

W<sup>m</sup> Harp
Notary Public.
My Commission expires
Jan 24-1906

---

### AFFIDAVIT OF ATTENDING PHYSICIAN OR MID-WIFE.

UNITED STATES OF AMERICA, Indian Territory, ⎫
      Southern            DISTRICT. ⎭

I,    Sallie Bond      , a    Midwife      , on oath state that I attended on
Mrs.   Marion Frazier      , wife of    Hudson Frazier      on the   27<sup>th</sup>   day of
December      , 1903; that there was born to her on said date a      female      child; that
said child was living March 4, 1905, and is said to have been named    Ruth Frazier

94

her<br>
Sallie x Bond<br>
mark

Witnesses To Mark:
⎧ CP Baker
⎩ R Bond

Subscribed and sworn to before me this   25th  day of     Sept       , 1905

*(Name Illegible)*
Notary Public.
My Com expires April 11<sup>th</sup> 1908

---

7-4228

Muskogee, Indian Territory, April 12, 1905.

Hudson Frazier,
         Arthur, Indian Territory.

Dear Sir:

Receipt is hereby acknowledged of the affidavits of Miriam Frazier and J. L. Wharton to the birth of Ruth Frazier daughter of Hudson and Miriam Frazier, December 27, 1903.

It is stated in the affidavit of the mother that she is a citizen by blood of the Choctaw Nation.  If this is correct you are requested to state under what name she was enrolled, the names of her parents, and if she has selected an allotment of the lands of the Choctaw and Chickasaw Nations give her roll number as it appears on her certificate of allotment.

Respectfully,

Commissioner in Charge.

---

Muskogee, Indian Territory, May 31, 1905.

Hudson Frazier,
         Duncan, Indian Territory.

Dear Sir:

Referring to the application for the enrollment of your child, Ruth Frazier, a letter was addressed to you on April 15, 1905, asking information which would enable us to identify the mother of this child upon  our records.

# Applications for Enrollment of Choctaw Newborn
## Act of 1905  Volume XX

Before further consideration can be given this application it will be necessary that you give the name under which your wife, Miriam Frazier, was enrolled, the name of her parents, and if she has selected an allotment of the lands of the Choctaw or Chickasaw Nation, give her roll number as the same appears upon her allotment certificate.

Respectfully,

[sic]

------------

*(The letter below typed as given.)*

Arthur, Indian Territory, Aug. 28 A.D 1905.

Commission to the Five Civilized Tribes,

Dear Sir:

My wife's roll number is 11789, her fathers name is Martin Charleston she get the land at Chickasaw Nation.

I have forgotten about this, I am sorry, please excuse me, so will you please send me of my child prove it. If its prove. I want hear from you, soon.

This is all, yours,

Hudson Frazier

Marian Frazier.

------------

7-NB-1499.

Muskogee, Indian Territory, September 1, 1905.

Hudson Frazier,
    Arthur, Indian Territory.

Dear Sir:

Receipt is hereby acknowledged of your letter of the 28th instant giving information relative to the enrollment of your wife as a citizen by blood of the Choctaw Nation in the matter of the application made by you for the enrollment of your infant child, Ruth Frazier.

In reply thereto, you are advised that the information contained in your letter has enabled this office to identify your wife upon its records as a citizen by blood of the Choctaw Nation.

You are further informed that in the application, for the enrollment of your child heretofore filed in this office, the date of birth is given in the application as December 27, 1903, while in the affidavit of the mother and attending physician the date of birth is given as December 27, 1905. The former date is apparently correct.

You are further advised that the mother's affidavit is signed Marian Frazier, while it appears from the records of this office that her given name is Marion.

There is inclosed you herewith for execution application for the enrollment of your infant child, Ruth Frazier, which is prepared to cover the case.  The mother in executing her affidavit should sign her given name Marion as it appears upon the records of this office.  You are requested to have the affidavits properly executed and returned to this office immediately, as no further action relative to the enrollment of your said child can be taken until the information requested is furnished.

Respectfully,

VR. 1-5.                                                           Commissioner.

_____

7-NB-1499

Muskogee, Indian Territory, October 10, 1905.

Hudson Frazier,
    Duncan, Indian Territory.

Dear Sir:

Receipt is hereby acknowledged of your letter of September 25, 1905, enclosing the affidavits of Marion Frazier and Sallie Bond to the birth of Ruth Frazier, daughter of Hudson and Marion Frazier, December 27, 1903, and the same have been filed in the matter of the enrollment of said child.

Respectfully,

Commissioner.

_____

# Applications for Enrollment of Choctaw Newborn
## Act of 1905   Volume XX

7-NB-1499

Muskogee, Indian Territory, October 31, 1905.

Hudson Frazier,
    Arthur, Indian Territory.

Dear Sir:

Receipt is hereby acknowledged of your letter of October 26, 1905, asking if the enrollment of your child Ruth Frazier has been approved.

In reply to your letter you are advised that the name of your child Ruth Frazier has not yet been placed upon a schedule of citizens by blood of the Choctaw Nation prepared for forwarding to the Secretary of the Interior.

In event further evidence is necessary to enable this office to pass upon the right of this child to enrollment, you will be duly notified.

Respectfully,

Commissioner.

---

7-NB-1499

Muskogee, Indian Territory, January 18, 1906.

Hudson Frazier,
    Arthur, Indian Territory.

Dear Sir:

Receipt is hereby acknowledged of your letter of January 11, 1906, asking if your child Ruth Frazier has been enrolled; you also state that you have a child born November 28, 1905, named John Frazier and you desire to be informed if he can be enrolled.

In reply to your letter you are advised that the name of your child Ruth Frazier has not yet been placed upon a schedule of new born citizens of the Choctaw Nation, but it is probable that her name will be placed upon the next schedule so prepared.  You will be advised when her enrollment is approved by the Department.

You are further advised, relative to the enrollment of your child John Frazier, born November 28, 1905, that under the act of Congress approved March 3, 1905, there is no provision for the enrollment of children born subsequent to March , 1905.

Respectfully,

Commissioner.

---

*(The letter below belongs with Applicant #1497 - Joseph James Wright.)*

7-NB-1499

Muskogee, Indian Territory, December 10, 1906.

Mansfield, McMurray & Cornish,
    Attorneys for Choctaw and Chickasaw Nations,
        South McAlester, Indian Territory.

Gentlemen:

You are hereby advised that on November 24, 1906, the Department rescinded its action of January 2, 1906, and returned the record in the matter of the enrollment of Joseph James Wright as a new born citizen of the Choctaw Nation under the Act March 3, 1905 for reconsideration in accordance with the provisions of Section 2 of the Act of Congress approved April 26, 1906.

Respectfully,

Acting Commissioner.

---

*(The letter below belongs with Applicant #1497 - Joseph James Wright.)*

7-NB-1497

Muskogee, Indian Territory, December 10, 1906.

E. H. Wright,
    Stewart, Indian Territory.

Dear Sir:

You are hereby advised that on November 24, 1906 the Department rescinded its action of January 2, 1906, and returned the record in the matter of the application for the enrollment of Joseph James Wright as a new born citizen of the Choctaw Nation under the Act of Congress approved March 3, 1905 for reconsideration in accordance with the provisions of Section 2 of The Act of Congress approved April 26, 1906.

You are therefore requested to forward new affidavits to the birth of your child Joseph James Wright on the blank inclosed herewith which affidavits should show that the child was living March 4, 1906.

Please give this matter immediate attention.

Respectfully,

B. C.                                                                    Acting Commissioner.

---

Choc. New Born 1500
    Eliza Jane Jennings
    (Born March 21, 1905)

1500

# NEW BORN
## CHOCTAW
### ENROLLMENT

ELIZA JANE JENNINGS

(BORN MARCH 21, 1905)

As Citizen of the
CHOCTAW NATION
Act of Congress
Approved March 3, 1905

CANCELLED

RECORD TRANSFERRED TO CHOCTAW
NEW BORN #636

ACT OF CONGRESS APPROVED APRIL 26, 1906.
JULY 13, 1906

**1500**

# CHOCTAW          1500

## NEW BORN

ACT OF CONGRESS APPROVED MARCH 30, 1905.

*Eliza Jane Jennings*
*(Born March 21, 1905)*

# CANCELLED

*Record transferred to*
*Choctaw New Born #636*

ACT OF CONGRESS APPROVED APRIL 26, 1906.

**JUL 13 1906**

---

Choc. New Born 1501
  Nancy Welsh
  (Born July 5, 1905)

1501

## NEW BORN
### CHOCTAW
### ENROLLMENT

NANCY WELSH

(BORN JULY 5, 1905)

As Citizen of the
CHOCTAW NATION
Act of Congress
Approved March 3, 1905

TRANSFERRED TO CHOCTAW N.B. (APRIL 26,
1906) NO.897
OCTOBER 24, 1906

**1501**

---

101

# CHOCTAW  1501

## NEW BORN

ACT OF CONGRESS APPROVED MARCH 30, 1905.

*Nancy Welsh*
*Born July 5, 1905.*

*Transferred to Choctaw*
*N. B. (Apl 26 1906)*
*No. 897*  **OCT 24 1906**

---

Choc. New Born 1502
    Winter Kelly Spring
    *(Birthdate not given.)*

1502

## NEW BORN
### CHOCTAW
### ENROLLMENT

WINTER KELLY SPRING

As Citizen of the
CHOCTAW NATION
Act of Congress
Approved March 3, 1905

C A N C E L L E D

RECORD TRANSFERRED TO CHOCTAW
NEW BORN NO. 569.

ACT OF CONGRESS APPROVED APRIL 26, 1906/

JUNE 30, 1906.
### 1502

---

# CHOCTAW

1502

## NEW BORN

ACT OF CONGRESS APPROVED MARCH 30, 1905.

*Winter Kelly Spring*

# CANCELLED

*Record transferred to*

CHOCTAW   NEW BORN *No 569*

ACT OF CONGRESS APPROVED APRIL 26, 1906.

*June 30, 1906.*

---

Choc. New Born 1503
Odis Atchison Kiefer
(Born Sep. 9, 1903)

---

1503

## NEW BORN

### CHOCTAW
### ENROLLMENT

ODIS ATCHISON KIEFER.

(BORN SEPTEMBER 9, 1903)

As Citizen of the
CHOCTAW NATION
Act of Congress
Approved March 3, 1905

CANCELLED

RECORD TRANSFERRED TO CHOCTAW
NEW BORN 788.
ACT OF CONGRESS APPROVED APRIL 26, 1906.

JULY 20, 1906

**1503**

# CHOCTAW   1503

## NEW BORN

ACT OF CONGRESS APPROVED MARCH 30, 1905.

*Odis Atchison Kiefer*
*(Born Sept. 9, 1903)*

# CANCELLED

*Record transferred to*
*Choctaw New Born 788*

ACT OF CONGRESS APPROVED APRIL 26, 1906.

**JUL 20 1906**

---

Choc. New Born 1504
 Joseph Alexander
 (Born June 13, 1903)

1504

## NEW BORN
### CHOCTAW
### ENROLLMENT

JOSEPH ALEXANDER

(BORN JUNE 13, 1903)

As Citizen of the
CHOCTAW NATION
Act of Congress
Approved March 3, 1905

CANCELLED

TRANSFERRED TO CHOCTAW NEW BORN NO. 740

104

ACT OF CONGRESS APPROVED APRIL 26, 1906.
AUGUST 17, 1906

## 1504

---

# CHOCTAW                    1504

## NEW BORN

ACT OF CONGRESS APPROVED MARCH 30, 1905.

*Joseph Alexander*

*(Born June 13, 1903)*

# CANCELLED

*Transferred to Choctaw*
*Newborn No. 740.*

ACT OF CONGRESS APPROVED APRIL 26, 1906.

**AUG 17 1906**

---

Choc. New Born 1505
     Maudie Bell Freeman
     (Born Feb. 18, 1904)

---

1505

## NEW BORN
### CHOCTAW
### ENROLLMENT

MAUDIE BELL FREEMAN

(BORN FEBRUARY 18, 1904)

As Citizen of the
CHOCTAW NATION
Act of Congress
Approved March 3, 1905

CANCELLED

RECORD TRANSFERRED TO CHOCTAW NEW BORN #499

ACT OF CONGRESS APPROVED APRIL 26, 1906.

JULY 13, 1906

**1505**

---

# CHOCTAW   1505

## NEW BORN

ACT OF CONGRESS APPROVED MARCH 30, 1905.

*Maudie Bell Freeman
(Born Feb. 18, 1904)*

# CANCELLED

*Record transferred to
Choctaw New Born #498*

ACT OF CONGRESS APPROVED APRIL 26, 1906.

**JUL 13 1906**

---

Choc. New Born 1506
   Dixen Ludlow
(Born Aug. 15, 1903)

---

**1506**

## NEW BORN
CHOCTAW
ENROLLMENT

DIXEN LUDLOW

(BORN AUGUST 15, 1903)

106

As Citizen of the
CHOCTAW NATION
Act of Congress
Approved March 3, 1905

CANCELLED

RECORD TRANSFERRED TO CHOCTAW NEW BORN #559

ACT OF CONGRESS APPROVED APRIL 26, 1906.
JULY 13, 1906

## 1506

---

# CHOCTAW          1506

## NEW BORN

ACT OF CONGRESS APPROVED MARCH 30, 1905.

*Dixen Ludlow*
*(Born August 15, 1903)*

# CANCELLED

*Record transferred to*
*Choctaw New Born #559*
ACT OF CONGRESS APPROVED APRIL 26, 1906.

**JUL 13 1906**

---

Choc. New Born 1507
Ida May McClure
(Born April 8, 1905)

---

BIRTH AFFIDAVIT.

### DEPARTMENT OF THE INTERIOR.
### COMMISSION TO THE FIVE CIVILIZED TRIBES.

---

IN RE APPLICATION FOR ENROLLMENT, as a citizen of the      Choctaw      Nation, of
Ida May M$^c$Clure      , born on the  8   day of   April   , 1905

Name of Father:  Garrett T. McClure          a citizen of the   Choctaw     Nation.

Name of Mother:  Mary E. McClure          a citizen of the   ~~Choctaw~~ *non*     Nation.

Postoffice      Cameron Ind. Ter.

---

### AFFIDAVIT OF MOTHER.

UNITED STATES OF AMERICA, Indian Territory, ⎤
    Central        DISTRICT. ⎦

    I,   Mary E M$^c$Clure   , on oath state that I am   19   years of age and a citizen
by   ~~marriage~~   , of the     U.S. ~~Choctaw~~    Nation; that I am the lawful wife of
Garrett T. M$^c$Clure      , who is a citizen, by  Blood      of the      Choctaw
Nation; that a    Female    child was born to me on   8th   day of   April      , 1905;
that said child has been named    Ida May M$^c$Clure    , and was living ~~March 4~~, 1905.
                                               *April 18,*

                    Mary E. M$^c$Clure

Witnesses To Mark:

    Subscribed and sworn to before me this  21  day of    April     , 1905

                    *(Name Illegible)*
                    Notary Public.

---

### AFFIDAVIT OF ATTENDING PHYSICIAN OR MID-WIFE.

UNITED STATES OF AMERICA, Indian Territory, ⎤
    Central        DISTRICT. ⎦

    I,   M.W. Harrison   , a  Physician    , on oath state that I attended on
Mrs.  Mary E. McClure   , wife of   Garrett T McClure    on the  8  day of April,
1905; that there was born to her on said date a    female    child; that said child was
living ~~March 4~~, 1905, and is said to have been named   Ida May McClure
*April 19*

                    M.W. Harrison M.D.

Witnesses To Mark:

{

    Subscribed and sworn to before me this 21 day of    April    , 1905

*(Name Illegible)*
Notary Public.

7-2297

Muskogee, Indian Territory, April 26, 1905.

Garrett T. McClure,
    Cameron, Indian Territory.

Dear Sir:

    Receipt is hereby acknowledged of the affidavits of Mary E. McClure and M. W. Harrison, to the birth of Ida May McClure, child of Garrett T. and Mary E. McClure, April 8, 1905.

    You are advised that under the provisions of the Act of Congress, approved March 3, 1905, the Commission is authorized for a period of sixty days from that date, to receive applications for enrollment of children born to enrolled citizens by blood of the Choctaw Nation, prior to March 4, 1905, and living on this date. You will therefore see that the Commission is without authority to enroll children born subsequent to March 4, 1905.

Respectfully,

Chairman.

Choc. New Born 1508
    Anna May McClure
    (Born March 5, 1905)

BIRTH AFFIDAVIT.

# DEPARTMENT OF THE INTERIOR,
### COMMISSION TO THE FIVE CIVILIZED TRIBES.

---

**In Re Application for Enrollment,** as a citizen of the    Choctaw    Nation,
of  Anna May M$^c$Clure  , born on the    5$^{th}$    day of    March    , 1905

Name of Father: Napoleon B. M$^c$Clure          a citizen of the  Choctaw    Nation.

*intermarried*

Name of Mother: Maydell McClure          a citizen of the    Choctaw    Nation.

Post-office          Bennington I.T.

---

### AFFIDAVIT OF MOTHER.

---

UNITED STATES OF AMERICA, ⎫
  INDIAN TERRITORY,           ⎬
  Central          District. ⎭

I,  Maydell M$^c$Clure  , on oath state that I am    26    years of age and a
citizen by    Marriage    , of the    Choctaw    Nation; that I am the lawful wife of
Napoleon B. M$^c$Clure  , who is a citizen, by  Blood of the    Choctaw    Nation; that
a  Female    child was born to me on  5$^{th}$    day of    March  , 1905 , that said child
has been named    Anna May M$^c$Clure  , and is now living.

Maydell M$^c$Clure
WITNESSES TO MARK:

Subscribed and sworn to before me this  29$^{th}$    day of    March  , 1905.

C.C. M$^c$Clard
NOTARY PUBLIC.

---

### AFFIDAVIT OF ATTENDING PHYSICIAN OR MID-WIFE.

---

UNITED STATES OF AMERICA, ⎫
  INDIAN TERRITORY,           ⎬
  Central          District. ⎭

I,    B. M. Stark          , as    Midwife          , on oath state that I
attended on Mrs.  Maydell McClure    , wife of    Napoleon B. McClure    on the
5$^{th}$ day of    March    , 1905 ; that there was born to her on said date a    Female

child; that said child is now living and is said to have been named   Anna May M<sup>c</sup>Clure

B.M. Stark

**WITNESSES TO MARK:**

Subscribed and sworn to before me this   29<sup>th</sup>   day of   March   , 1905.

C.C. M<sup>c</sup>Clard
NOTARY PUBLIC.

---

Choc. New Born 1509
  Sam Crowder
  (Born Apr. 18, 1905)

1509

# NEW BORN
## CHOCTAW
### ENROLLMENT

SAM CROWDER

(BORN APRIL 18, 1905)

As Citizen of the
CHOCTAW NATION
Act of Congress
Approved March 3, 1905

CANCELLED

RECORD TRANSFERRED TO CHOCTAW NEW BORN #254

ACT OF CONGRESS APPROVED APRIL 26, 1906.
JULY 12, 1906

1509

# CHOCTAW  1509

## NEW BORN

ACT OF CONGRESS APPROVED MARCH 30, 1905.

*Sam Crowder*

*(Born April 18, 1905)*

# CANCELLED

*Record transferred to*
*Choctaw New Born #254.*

ACT OF CONGRESS APPROVED APRIL 26, 1906.

**JUL 13 1906**

---

Choc. New Born 1510
    Jodie Belvin
    (Born April 28, 1904)

1510

## NEW BORN
### CHOCTAW
### ENROLLMENT

JODIE BELVIN

(BORN APRIL 28, 1904)

As Citizen of the
CHOCTAW NATION
Act of Congress
Approved March 3, 1905

G R A N T E D

FEBRUARY 18, 1907

**1510**

112

# Applications for Enrollment of Choctaw Newborn
## Act of 1905   Volume XX

DEPARTMENT OF THE INTERIOR,
COMMISSIONER TO THE FIVE CIVILIZED TRIBES.

-----

In the matter of the application for the enrollment as a citizen by blood of the
Choctaw Nation of . . . . . . . . . . .

JODIE BELVIN............7-NB-1510.

-----

BIRTH AFFIDAVIT.

### DEPARTMENT OF THE INTERIOR.
### COMMISSION TO THE FIVE CIVILIZED TRIBES.

-----

IN RE APPLICATION FOR ENROLLMENT, as a citizen of the          Choctaw          Nation, of
Jodie Belvin          , born on the  28   day of  Apr   , 1904

Name of Father: Stephen Belvin          a citizen of the   Choctaw     Nation.
Name of Mother: Elsie Belvin          a citizen of the          "          Nation.

Postoffice          Boswell I.T.

-----

AFFIDAVIT OF MOTHER.

UNITED STATES OF AMERICA, Indian Territory, ⎤
   Cent          DISTRICT. ⎦

I,   Elsie Belvin      , on oath state that I am   24      years of age and a citizen by
blood    , of the   Choctaw     Nation; that I am the lawful wife of   Stephen Belvin   ,
who is a citizen, by  blood      of the          Choctaw          Nation; that a          Female
child was born to me on   28$^{th}$     day of     April      , 1904; that said child has been
named    Jodie Belvin      , and was living March 4, 1905.

Elsie Belvin

Witnesses To Mark:
⎧
⎨
⎩

Subscribed and sworn to before me this  5$^{th}$  day of   May      , 1905

B.W. Williams
Notary Public.

-----

# Applications for Enrollment of Choctaw Newborn
## Act of 1905   Volume XX

### AFFIDAVIT OF ATTENDING PHYSICIAN OR MID-WIFE.

UNITED STATES OF AMERICA, Indian Territory, ⎫
    Cent              DISTRICT. ⎬

I, Marguratt[sic] Whitlow , a   Midwife   , on oath state that I attended on Mrs.   Elsie Belvin   , wife of   Stephen Belvin   on the   28$^{th}$   day of   April   , 1904; that there was born to her on said date a     Female     child; that said child was living March 4, 1905, and is said to have been named   Jodie Belvin

Margreertte[sic] Whitlow

Witnesses To Mark:

  ⎰

Subscribed and sworn to before me this   5$^{th}$   day of   May   , 1905

B.W. Williams
Notary Public.

---

7-NB-1510

Muskogee, Indian Territory, October 29, 1906.

Stephen Belvin,
    Bennington, Indian Territory.

Dear Sir:

In the matter of the application for the enrollment of your child Jodie Belvin born April 28, 1904, you are requested to advise this office if this child is now living and if so please forward affidavit to his birth on the blank herewith inclosed.

This matter should receive immediate attention in order that disposition may be made of the application for the enrollment of said child.

Respectfully,

Commissioner.

---

7-N.B.-1510
O.L.J.

DEPARTMENT OF THE INTERIOR,
COMMISSIONER TO THE FIVE CIVILIZED TRIBES.

-----

In the matter of the application for the enrollment of Jodie Belvin as a citizen by blood of the Choctaw Nation.

DECISION.

It appears from the record herein that application was duly made for the enrollment of Jodie Belvin as a citizen by blood of the Choctaw Nation within the time limited by the provisions of Section One of The Act of Congress approved April 26, 1906 (34 Stats., 137).

It further appears from the record herein and from the records in the possession of this office that said applicant was born April 28, 1904, and is the daughter of Stephen N. Belvin and Elsie Belvin, whose names appear opposite Nos. 11479 and 11480, respectively, upon the final roll of citizens by blood of the Choctaw Nation approved by the Secretary of the Interior March 10, 1903; and that said applicant was living on March 4, 1905.

I am, therefore, of the opinion that Jodie Belvin should be enrolled as a citizen by blood of the Choctaw Nation, under the provisions of The Act of Congress approved March 3, 1905 (33 Stats., 1060), and it is so ordered.

Tams Bixby  Commissioner.

Muskogee, Indian Territory.
FEB 18 1907

---

7-NB-1510

COPY

Muskogee, Indian Territory, February 23, 1907.

Stephen Belvin,
   Bennington, Indian Territory.

Dear Sir:

Inclosed herewith you will find a copy of the decision of the Commissioner to the Five Civilized Tribes, rendered February 23, 1907, granting the application for the enrollment of Jodia[sic] Belvin as a citizen by blood of the Choctaw Nation.

You are further advised that the name of Jodie Belvin granted in said decision has been placed upon a schedule of citizens by blood of the Choctaw Nation to be submitted to the Secretary of the Interior for his approval.  You will be notified of Departmental action thereon.

Respectfully,

SIGNED

*Tams Bixby*

Registered.

Incl. 7-NB-1510.

Commissioner.

---

7-NB-1510

**COPY**

Muskogee, Indian Territory, February 23, 1907.

Mansfield, McMurray & Cornish,
    Attorneys for Choctaw and Chickasaw Nations,
        South McAlester, Indian Territory.

Gentlemen:

Inclosed herewith you will find a copy of the decision of the Commissioner to the Five Civilized Tribes, rendered February 23, 1907, granting the application for the enrollment of Jodie Belvin as a citizen by blood of the Choctaw Nation.

You are further advised that the name of Jodie Belvin granted in said decision has been placed upon a schedule of citizens by blood of the Choctaw Nation to be submitted to the Secretary of the Interior for his approval.  You will be notified of Departmental action thereon.

Respectfully,

SIGNED

*Tams Bixby*

Registered.

Incl. 7-NB-1510.

Commissioner.

---

*aB*

REFER IN REPLY TO THE FOLLOWING:

7-NB-1510

DEPARTMENT OF THE INTERIOR,
COMMISSIONER TO THE FIVE CIVILIZED TRIBES.

Muskogee, Indian Territory, March 28, 1907.

Elsie Belvin,
    Bennington, Indian Territory.

Dear Madam:

You are hereby advised that on March 2, 1907, the Secretary of the Interior approved the enrollment of your minor child, Jodie Belvin as a new born citizen of the Choctaw Nation, under the Act of Congress approved March 3, 1905, and her name appears upon the final roll of such citizens opposite No. 1582.

She is now entitled to an allotment, and application therefore should be made without delay at the Land Office for the Nation in which the prospective allotment is located.

Respectfully,

*(Name Illegible)*
Acting Commissioner.

_____

7-4098.

Muskogee, Indian Territory, May 15, 1905.

Stephen Belvin,
    Boswell, Indian Territory.

Dear Sir:

Receipt is hereby acknowledged of the affidavits of Elsie Belvin and Margret Whitlow to the birth of Jodie Belvin, daughter of Stephen and Elsie Belvin, April 28, 1904.

These affidavits were received at this office May 10, 1905, in an envelope postmarked Bennington, Indian Territory, May 9, 1905. You are advised that under the provisions of the act of Congress approved March 3, 1905, the Commission was authorized for a period of sixty days from that date to receive applications for the enrollment of children born to enrolled citizens by blood of the Choctaw and Chickasaw Nations prior to March 4, 1905.

The sixty days provided in this case expired May 2, 1905, and since that time the Commission is without authority to receive applications for the enrollment of citizens of the Choctaw and Chickasaw Nations.

Respectfully,

Chairman.

---

Choc. New Born 1511
> Eva Southard
> *(Birthdate not given.)*

1511

# NEW BORN
## CHOCTAW
### ENROLLMENT

EVA SOUTHARD

As Citizen of the
CHOCTAW NATION
Act of Congress
Approved March 3, 1905

C A N C E L L E D

RECORD TRANSFERRED TO CHOCTAW NEW BORN
#549

ACT OF CONGRESS APPROVED APRIL 26, 1906.
6-30-06.

1511

# CHOCTAW    1511

## NEW BORN

ACT OF CONGRESS APPROVED MARCH 30, 1905.

*Eva Southard*

# CANCELLED

*Record transferred to*

CHOCTAW    NEW BORN *No. 549*

ACT OF CONGRESS APPROVED APRIL 26, 1906.

*6-30-06*

---

Choc. New Born 1512
    Irene Mills
    (Born Sep. 5, 1904)

1512

## NEW BORN
### CHOCTAW
### ENROLLMENT

IRENE MILLS

(BORN SEPTEMBER 5, 1904)

As Citizen of the
CHOCTAW NATION
Act of Congress
Approved March 3, 1905

TRANSFERRED TO CHOCTAW N.B. APRIL 26, 1906
NO. 848

OCTOBER 24, 1906

## 1512

119

# NEW BORN   1512

## CHOCTAW

ACT OF CONGRESS APPROVED MARCH 30, 1905.

*Irene Mills*

*Born Sept 5 1904.*

*Transferred to Choctaw*
*N. B. Apr. 26 1906*
*No. 848*   **OCT 24 1906**

---

Choc. New Born 1513
 Ina Pearl Beal
 (Born Oct. 16, 1905)

---

1513

# NEW BORN

## CHOCTAW
### ENROLLMENT

### INA PEARL BEAL

(BORN OCTOBER 16, 1905)

As Citizen of the
CHOCTAW NATION
Act of Congress
Approved March 3, 1905

CANCELLED

RECORD TRANSFERRED TO CHOCTAW N.B. NO. 172

ACT OF CONGRESS APPROVED APRIL 26, 1906.
JULY 13, 1906

## 1513

---

# CHOCTAW 1513

## NEW BORN

ACT OF CONGRESS APPROVED MARCH 30, 1905.

*Ina Pearl Beal*

*(Born Oct 16, 1905)*

# CANCELLED

*Record transferred to Choc-
taw New Born No. 172*

ACT OF CONGRESS APPROVED APRIL 26, 1906.

**JUL 13 1906**

---

Choc. New Born 1514
Bertha Ellis Hayes
*(Birthdate not given.)*

1514

## NEW BORN
### CHOCTAW
### ENROLLMENT

BERTHA ELLIS HAYES

As Citizen of the
CHOCTAW NATION
Act of Congress
Approved March 3, 1905

CANCELLED

NEW AFFIDAVITS FILED UNDER ACT OF APRIL
26, 1906.

TRANSFERRED TO CHOCTAW NEW BORN (AC OF APRIL
26, 1906) #503.

JUNE 25, 1906

**1514**

121

# CHOCTAW   1514

## NEW BORN

ACT OF CONGRESS APPROVED MARCH 30, 1905.

*Bertha Ellis Hayes*

# CANCELLED

*New affidavits filed
under act of April 26, 1906.
Transferred to Choctaw New Born
(Act of April 26, 1906) #503.*

**JUN 25 1906**

---

Choc. New Born 1515
    Lula Myrtle Casey
    (Born Dec. 22, 1905)

1515

## NEW BORN
CHOCTAW
ENROLLMENT

LULA MYRTLE CASEY
(BORN DECEMBER 22, 1905)

As Citizen of the
CHOCTAW NATION
Act of Congress
Approved March 3, 1905

TRANSFERRED TO CHOCTAW N.B. (APRIL 26, 1906
NO. 910.

OCTOBER 24, 1906

**1515**

122

# NEW BORN                    1515

## CHOCTAW

ACT OF CONGRESS APPROVED MARCH 30, 1905.

*Lula Myrtle Casey.*
*Born Dec. 22 1905*

*Transferred to Choctaw*
*N.B. (Apr. 26, 1906)*
*No. 910*        **OCT 24 1906**

---

Choc. New Born 1516
　　Millie Pope
　　*(Birthdate not given.)*

1516

# NEW BORN

## CHOCTAW

### ENROLLMENT

MILLIE POPE

As Citizen of the
CHOCTAW NATION
Act of Congress
Approved March 3, 1905

C A N C E L L E D

AND RECORD TRANSFERRED TO CHOCTAW
NEW BORN 508.

ACT OF CONGRESS APPROVED APRIL 26, 1906.

**1516**

---

# CHOCTAW    1516

# NEW BORN

ACT OF CONGRESS APPROVED MARCH 30, 1905.

*Millie Pope*

# CANCELLED

*and record transferred*

To CHOCTAW    NEW BORN *508*.

ACT OF CONGRESS APPROVED APRIL 26, 1906.

---

Choc. New Born 1517
    Horace Allen
    (Born Jan. 13, 1906)

BIRTH AFFIDAVIT.

### DEPARTMENT OF THE INTERIOR.
### COMMISSION TO THE FIVE CIVILIZED TRIBES.

IN RE APPLICATION FOR ENROLLMENT, as a citizen of the    Choctaw    Nation, of
Horrice[sic] Allen    , born on the  13  day of   January  , 1906

Name of Father:  W B Allen                  a citizen of the   Choctaw   Nation.
Name of Mother:  Bertha Allen               a citizen of the   Choctaw   Nation.

Postoffice    Eastman Ind Ter

---

AFFIDAVIT OF MOTHER.

UNITED STATES OF AMERICA, Indian Territory,
    Southern            DISTRICT.

I,  Bertha Allen    , on oath state that I am    16    years of age and a citizen by
Intermarriage    , of the    Choctaw    Nation; that I am the lawful wife of    W B
Allen    , who is a citizen, by  Blood    of the    Choctaw    Nation; that a
male    child was born to me on   13    day of   January    , 1906; that said child has
been named    Horrice Allen    , and was living ~~March 4~~, 1906.

*Jan 13*

124

# Applications for Enrollment of Choctaw Newborn
## Act of 1905   Volume XX

Bertha Allen

Witnesses To Mark:
{ Lou Shipman
{ Nellie Shipman

Subscribed and sworn to before me this  13  day of    Jan      , 1906

J K Allen
Notary Public.

---

**AFFIDAVIT OF ATTENDING PHYSICIAN OR MID-WIFE.**

UNITED STATES OF AMERICA, Indian Territory, }
   Southern                  **DISTRICT.** }

I,    L E Hall          , a      State         , on oath state that I attended on
Mrs.  Bertha Allen       , wife of  W.B. Allen      on the 13  day of     January   ,
1906; that there was born to her on said date a    male    child; that said child was living
*Jan 13*, 1906, and is said to have been named  Horrice Allen
her mark
L E  x  Hall

Witnesses To Mark:
{ Lou Shipman
{ Nellie Shipman

Subscribed and sworn to before me this  13  day of    Jan      , 1906

J K Allen
Notary Public.

---

Choc. New Born 1518
Edith Turnbull
(Born Jan. 23, 1906)

---

1518

# NEW BORN
## CHOCTAW
ENROLLMENT

EDITH TURNBULL

(BORN JANUARY 23, 1906)

As Citizen of the
CHOCTAW NATION
Act of Congress
Approved March 3, 1905

TO N.B. (ACT OF APRIL 26, 1906)
NO. 157

DECEMBER 10, 1906

## 1518

---

*Choctaw N.B.   1518*

*Edith Turnbull
born Jan. 23, 1906*

*To N.B. (Act of Apl 26, 1906)
No. 157
Dec. 10, 1906.*

---

Choc. New Born 1519
    Irene Dyer
    (Born Oct. 1, 1903)

---

1519

# NEW BORN
## CHOCTAW
### ENROLLMENT

IRENE DYER

(BORN OCTOBER 1, 1903)

As Citizen of the
CHOCTAW NATION
Act of Congress
Approved March 3, 1905

CANCELLED

RECORD TRANSFERRED TO CHOCTAW
NEW BORN NO. 711.

ACT OF CONGRESS APPROVED APRIL 26, 1906.
JULY 13, 1906

1519

---

# CHOCTAW     1519
## NEW BORN
ACT OF CONGRESS APPROVED MARCH 30, 1905.

*Irene Dyer*
*(Born Oct. 1, 1903)*

# CANCELLED
*Record transferred to Choctaw New Born No. 711*
ACT OF CONGRESS APPROVED APRIL 26, 1906.

**JUL 13 1906**

Choc. New Born 1520
>   Dock Nail
>   (Born March 27, 1903)

*1520*

*Application*
*New Born*
*for Enrollment of*
*Dock Nail*
*(Born March 27, 1903)*

*New Born*

*As a citizen of the*
*Choctaw Nation*
*Act of Congress approved*
*March 3, 1905*

*Granted*
*Mar. 14-1906*

*No.*   3315                          FORM NO. 598.

# MARRIAGE LICENSE.

UNITES STATES OF AMERICA, ⎫
  THE INDIAN TERRITORY,      ⎬ ss:
  Central            DISTRICT. ⎭

**To any Person Authorized by Law to Solemnize Marriage—Greeting:**

*You are hereby commanded to solemnize the Rite and publish the* **Banns of Matrimony** *between*
*Mr.*   James Nail                          *of*   Blanco          *in*
*the Indian Territory, aged*  36  *years, and Mrs* Jane Tucker    *of*   Blanco        *in the*
*Indian Territory, aged*   3?   *years, according to law, and do you officially sign and return this License to the*
*parties therein named.*

128

# Applications for Enrollment of Choctaw Newborn
## Act of 1905   Volume XX

*WITNESS my hand and official seal, this*   23   *day of*   Dec   *A. D.* 1902

EJ Fannin
*Clerk of the United States Court.*

JM Dodge      *Deputy*

---

# CERTIFICATE OF MARRIAGE.

UNITES STATES OF AMERICA, ⎫
   THE INDIAN TERRITORY,   ⎬ ss:
_____ DISTRICT. ⎭

I,   E D Cameron
*a*   Minister of the Gospel

*do hereby CERTIFY, that on the*   23rd   *day of*   Dec      *A, D.* 190 2 ; *I did duly and according to law, as commanded in the foregoing License, solemnize the Rite and publish the BANNS OF MATRIMONY between the parties therein named.*

*Witness my hand this* 23rd   *day of*   Dec   , *A. D.* 190 2

*My credentials are recorded in the office of the Clerk of the United States Court in the Indian Territory, Central District, Book*   C   *Page* 3

E.D. Cameron
*a*  Minister of the Gospel

---

DELINQUENT AFFIDAVIT
   NO._____

# CHOCTAW ENROLLING COMMISSION.

IN THE MATTER OF THE ENROLLMENT OF          Doctor Nail

, a delinquent, who is a citizen of the          Choctaw
Nation by    blood

### AFFIDAVIT OF DELINQUENT.

Jimmie Nail                    , being duly sworn, states that he is a citizen of
the   Choctaw      Nation, and that he is a    the Father      of   Doctor Nail
who is a citizen of the    Choctaw      Nation, whose name appears upon the final roll as
approved by the Honorable Secretary of the Interior      ~~My~~          said enrollment

129

# Applications for Enrollment of Choctaw Newborn
## Act of 1905   Volume XX

number being   13083   . This affiant further states that he is related to the following citizens
of the   Choctaw      Nation, to wit:

| | | |
|---|---|---|
| Alford Nail   Father | , enrollment No. _____ |
| Kissen Reed   Uncle | , enrollment No. _____ |
| Ellen Cole   Aunt | , enrollment No. _____ |

Affiant further states that as such relative of the above named persons he is entitled to
enrollment and to share in the division of the property of said   Choctaw Indian  Tribe.

WITNESSETH:

Must be two        Alfred W M$^c$Clure
witnesses who                                        Jimmie Nail
are citizens.      J.W. White

Subscribed and sworn to before me this _____ day of
_____ 190__

_____ Notary Public.

My Commission Expires:

_____

BIRTH AFFIDAVIT.

## DEPARTMENT OF THE INTERIOR,
### COMMISSION TO THE FIVE CIVILIZED TRIBES.

_____

**In Re Application for Enrollment,** as a citizen of the   Choctaw    Nation,
of   Dock Nail  , born on the   27$^{th}$   day of   March   , 1902[sic]

Name of Father: Jimmie Nail                 a citizen of the  Choctaw    Nation.
Name of Mother: Becky Nail               a citizen of the   Choctaw    Nation.

Post-office      So M$^c$Alester

_____

**AFFIDAVIT OF MOTHER.**

_____

UNITED STATES OF AMERICA, ⎱
    INDIAN TERRITORY,
    Cent                    District. ⎰

I,   Becky Nail , on oath state that I am   26    years of age and a citizen by
intermarriage  , of the   Choctaw    Nation; that I am the lawful wife of   Jimmie
Nail, who is a citizen, by blood of the   Choctaw     Nation; that a   Mal[sic]
child was born to me on   27   day of   March   , 1902 , that said child has been
named   Dock   , and is now living.

130

# Applications for Enrollment of Choctaw Newborn
## Act of 1905  Volume XX

her
Becky  x  Nail

mark

{ Wallace Wilkinson
M. R. Harris

Subscribed and sworn to before me this  30<sup>th</sup>  day of  April  , 1904.

E.P. Hill

NOTARY PUBLIC.

---

**AFFIDAVIT OF ATTENDING PHYSICIAN OR MID-WIFE.**

---

UNITED STATES OF AMERICA, ⎫
INDIAN TERRITORY, ⎬
Cent                    District. ⎭

I,   Nancy Coble       , a   house wife        , on oath state that I
attended on Mrs.   Becky Nail    , wife of   Jimmie Nail     on the   27  day of
March , 1902 ; that there was born to her on said date a    Male    child; that said
child is now living and is said to have been named  Dock Nail

her
Nancy  x  Coble

WITNESSES TO MARK: mark

{ Wallace Wilkinson
W<sup>m.</sup> C. Liedtke

Subscribed and sworn to before me this  4<sup>th</sup>  day of   May   , 1904.

WG Weimer

Commission expires August 8, 1905.                    NOTARY PUBLIC.

---

131

**NEW-BORN AFFIDAVIT.**

Number...............

## ...Choctaw Enrolling Commission...

———

IN THE MATTER OF THE APPLICATION FOR ENROLLMENT, as a citizen of the
Choctaw            Nation, of            Doc Nail

born on the  27<sup>th</sup>   day of __March__ 190 3

| | |
|---|---|
| Name of father    Jimmie Nail | a citizen of    Choctaw |
| Nation final enrollment No.  13083 | |
| Name of mother    Jane Nail | a citizen of    Choctaw |
| Nation final enrollment No.  —— | |

Postoffice       Blanco IT

### AFFIDAVIT OF MOTHER.

UNITED STATES OF AMERICA
INDIAN TERRITORY
  Central        DISTRICT

I        Jane Nail            , on oath state that I am
  30        years of age and ~~a citizen~~ by  white    of the _____Nation, and as
such have been placed upon the final roll of the _____ Nation, by the Honorable
Secretary of the Interior my final enrollment number being _____; that I am the lawful
wife of    Jimmie Nail     , who is a citizen of the    Choctaw      Nation, and as such has
been placed upon the final roll of said Nation by the Honorable Secretary of the Interior, his
final enrollment number being      13083    and that a    Male    child was born to me on the
27<sup>th</sup>   day of    Mch     190 3; that said child has been named   Doc Nail      , and is now
living.

Jane Nail

Witnesseth.

Must be two    ⎫  M.S. Clark
Witnesses who  ⎬
are Citizens.   ⎭   Henry Dailey

Subscribed and sworn to before me this    12<sup>th</sup>   day of   Jan      190 5

W.A. Shoney
Notary Public.

My commission expires:
    Jan 10, 1909

———

# Affidavit of Attending Physician or Midwife.

UNITED STATES OF AMERICA⎫
INDIAN TERRITORY          ⎬
  Central          DISTRICT ⎭

I,   Martha Dailey          a          midwife
on oath state that I attended on Mrs.   Jane Nail          wife of          Jimmie Nail
on the   27<sup>th</sup>   day of   March   , 190 3 , that there was born to her on said date a   Male
child, that said child is now living, and is said to have been named   Doc Nail

Martha Dailey   M.D.

Subscribed and sworn to before me this, the   12<sup>th</sup>   day of   Jan          190 5

W A Shoney
Notary Public.

WITNESSETH:

Must be two witnesses ⎧ Henry Dailey
who are citizens and  ⎨
know the child.       ⎩ M.S. Clark

We hereby certify that we are well acquainted with          Martha Dailey
a          midwife          and know   her          to be reputable and of good standing in the
community.

Henry Dailey
⎨
M.S. Clark

BIRTH AFFIDAVIT.

## DEPARTMENT OF THE INTERIOR.
## COMMISSION TO THE FIVE CIVILIZED TRIBES.

**IN RE APPLICATION FOR ENROLLMENT,** as a citizen of the          Choctaw          Nation, of
Dock Nail          , born on the   4<sup>th</sup>   day of   March   , 1902

Name of Father: Jimmie Nail                    a citizen of the   Choctaw   Nation.
Name of Mother: Beckie Nail                    a citizen of the United States ~~Nation~~.

Postoffice          Blanco, I T

133

# Applications for Enrollment of Choctaw Newborn
## Act of 1905   Volume XX

AFFIDAVIT OF MOTHER.

UNITED STATES OF AMERICA, Indian Territory, ⎫
  Central                              DISTRICT. ⎭

I,   Beckie Nail    , on oath state that I am   28   years of age and a citizen by intermarriage    , of the    Choctaw    Nation; that I am the lawful wife of   Jimmie Nail    , who is a citizen, by   blood    of the    Choctaw    Nation; that a male    child was born to me on   4"   day of   March    , 1902; that said child has been named   Dock Nail    , and was living March 4, 1905.

                                                  her
                                        Beckie  x  Nail
Witnesses To Mark:                              mark
  ⎰ Alfred W McClure
  ⎱ Nebat N. Bonaparte

Subscribed and sworn to before me this   27"  day of   March    , 1905

                              E. P. Hill
                                  Notary Public.

_____

AFFIDAVIT OF ATTENDING PHYSICIAN OR MID-WIFE.

UNITED STATES OF AMERICA, Indian Territory, ⎫
  Central                              DISTRICT. ⎭

I,   Martha E Dailey          , a   mid wife      , on oath state that I attended on Mrs.  Beckie Nail      , wife of   Jimmie Nail    on the   4"  day of   March   , 1902; that there was born to her on said date a    Male    child; that said child was living March 4, 1905, and is said to have been named   Dock Nail

                          Martha E. Dailey
Witnesses To Mark:
  ⎰

Subscribed and sworn to before me this   23$^{rd}$    day of   March      , 1905

                              E. P. Hill
                                  Notary Public.

_____

134

United States of America,
Indian Territory, Central District.

  Jimmie Nail and Beckie Jane Nail, of Blanco, I. T., after being duly sworn, states that they are the mother and father of Dock Nail, an infant boy that he is the same for which application for enrollment has heretofore been made for enrollemnt[sic] as a citizen of the Choctaw Nation, affiants further say that they were married in December, 1902 and that their son Dock Nail was born on the 27th day of March, 1903, that the date in the affidavit heretofore made given the birth of said child in the year of 1902 was a mistake, that said child was born after affiants were married in December, 1902, that Nancy Cable and Martha Dailey were present at the birth of said child. That Dr. Butts, who has moved to some place near Ardmore, I. T. was the Dr. in attendance.

  Affiants further states ~~that~~ that that the name of the mother of the said child is Beckie Jane nail[sic] and that she is the same person whose name appears on said marriage license as Jane Tucker.

Jimmie Nail

Witness to Mark.

her<br>
Beckie Jane x Nail

D D Kushford

mark

Subscribed and sworn to before me this the   14<sup>th</sup>   day of October, 1905.

Martin Savage<br>
Notary Public.

My commission expires Feb 28-1909

---

Before the Hon Tams Bixby Commissioner to the<br>
Five civilized tribes in the Indian<br>
Territory- At Muskogee.

In Re :-
  Dock Nail, ~~applicant~~. a minor, by his father and Mother
  Jimmie and Becky Jane Nail, Applicant.
   Vs.

The Choctaw Nation.        *No 4937*

Respondent.

------------------------------------------------------------

APPLICATION FOR ENROLLMENT.

  Comes now Dock Nail, the above minor and appearing by his Father and Mother, Jimmie and Becky Jane Nail, moves the Hon Tams Bixby Commissioner to the Five civilized tribes, to enroll said Dock Nail as a member of the

Choctaw tribe of Indians and bases his right to enrollment upon the following grounds to wit :-

That on the 23,rd day of December 1902, the said Jimmie Nail a Choctaw Indian by blood, duly enrolled and recognized as such, was lawfully married to Becky Jane Tucker, a white woman, and that thereafter on the 27,th day of March 1903, there was born to the said Jimmie and Becky Jane Nail the issue of said marriage a male child, and which was named Dock Nail, and that said Dock Nail is the above named applicant who appears and makes application for enrollment herein.

Wherefore, they pray that the said Dock Nail e enrolled as a member of the Choctaw tribe of Indians, with all the rights priviliges[sic] and immunities as other members of said tribe.

Respectfully submitted on this the
29,th day of December 1905.

Dock Nail          Applicant,
per   Jimmie & Becky Nail

His Father and Mother
By    Preslie B. Cole
His attorney.

---

*(The affidavit below typed as given.)*

INDIAN TERRITORY,        )
                         )
CENTRAL DISTRICT.        )

### AFFIDAVIT OF JIMMIE NAIL.

Affiant Jimmie Nail being duly sworn deposes and says:-

My name is Jimmie Nail, I am a Choctaw Indian by blood and reside at Blanco, Ind. Ter. On the 23rd day of December 1902, I was lawfully married to Beckie Jane Tucker a white whoman, after having procured marriage license from the United States Court at South McAlester, Ind. Ter. On the 27th day of March 1903 there was born to me and my said wife, a male child which we named Dock Nail and which is now living and not enrolled. The marriage license referred to in the above were issued in the name of Jane Tucker as that is the name of my wife. Her full name is Becky Jane Nail. The Becky Nail refered to in the affidavit filed with the application for enrollment of Dock Nail in this matter, and Jane Tucker refered to in the marriage license is one and the same person, and is my wife, and is the mother of the said Dock Nail. The date of the birth of Dock Nail as set forth above is true and correct.

Jimmie Nail

Subscribed and sworn to before me this the  28  day of December 1905.

Martin Savage
Notary Public.

---

*(The affidavit below typed as given.)*

INDIAN TERRITORY, )
        )
CENTRAL DISTRICT. )

### AFFIDAVIT OF JANE NAIL.

Affiant Jane Nail being duly sworn deposes and says:

My name is Jane Nail, I am a white woman and reside at Blanco, Ind. Ter.  On the 23rd day of December 1902, I was lawfully married to Jimmie Nail a Choctaw Indian by blood, after having procured marriage license from the United States Court at South McAlester, Ind. Ter.  On the 27th day of March 1903 there was born to me and my said husband a male child whom we named Dock Nail and which is now living and not enrolled.  The marriage license refered to in the above was issued in the name of Jane Tucker and that was my name before marriage.  My full name is Becky Jane Nail.  The Becky Nail refered to in the ~~affidavit filed with~~ the application for enrollment of Dock Nail in this matter, and Jane Tucker refered to in the marriage license is one and the same person, and is my name, and I am the mother of the said Dock Nail.  The date of the birth of Dock Nail as set forth above is true and correct.  My name before marriage was Becky Jane Tucker, but the Clerk issued the License in the name of Jane Tucker.  I don't know how that happened as I was not present when they were issued.

               her
*Witness*        Becky  x  Jane Nail
*T L Grady*        mark
*M Savage*

Subscribed and sworn to before me this   28   day of December 1905.

Martin Savage
Notary Public.

---

# Applications for Enrollment of Choctaw Newborn
## Act of 1905   Volume XX

*(The affidavit below typed as given.)*

Before the Hon Tams Bixby, Commissioner to
The Five tribes of Indians-at Muskogee, Indian Territory
Indian Territory.

In Re,

> Dock Nail a minor by his father and mother
> Jimmie and Becky Nail
>
> Applicants
>
> Vs.
>
> The Choctaw Nation......................... Respondent.

PROOF OF SERVICE.

M F Winter    being duly sworn deposes and says :-

I caused a letter containing a true, perfect and literal copy of the within and foregoing Application *and affidavits* for enrollment, to be registered by the *(typing marked out)*, at the Post Master at South McAlester Indian Territory, on the 29th day of December 1905, in a letter addressed to Mansfield McMurray & Cornish, attorneys for the Choctaw and Chickasaw Nations at said South McAlester.  That a registry receipt therefor, is hereto attached and made a part hereof.

M.F. Winter

Subscribed and sworn to before me on this the 29, day of December 1905.
My commission expires on the  28  day of Feb  190 8    R.H. *(Illegible)*
Notary Public.

7-NB-1520.

### DEPARTMENT OF THE INTERIOR,
### COMMISSIONER TO THE FIVE CIVILIZED TRIBES.

In the matter of the application for the enrollment of Dock Nail as a citizen by blood of the Choctaw Nation.

### D E C I S I O N.

It appears from the record in this case that on March 28, 1905, there was filed with the Commission to the Five Civilized Tribes an application for the enrollment of Dock Nail as a citizen by blood of the Choctaw Nation.

It further appears from the record herein and from the records of the Commission to the Five Civilized Tribes that the applicant was born on March 27, 1903, and is a son of Jimmie Nail, a recognized and enrolled citizen by blood of the Choctaw Nation, whose name appears as number 13083 upon the final roll of citizens by blood of the Choctaw Nation approved by the Secretary of the Interior March 19, 1903, and Beckie Nail, a non-citizen white woman; and that said applicant was living on March 4, 1905.

The Act of Congress approved March 3, 1905 (33 Stats., 1070) provides:

"That the Commission to the Five Civilized Tribes is authorized for sixty days after the date of the approval of this act to receive and consider applications for enrollment of children born subsequent to September twenty-fifth, nineteen hundred and two, and prior to March fourth, nineteen hundred and five, and who were living on said latter date, to citizens by blood of the Choctaw and Chickasaw tribes of Indians whose enrollment has been approved by the Secretary of the Interior prior to the date of the approval of this act; and to enroll and make allotments to such children."

I am, therefore, of the opinion that Dock Nail should be enrolled as a citizen by blood of the Choctaw Nation in accordance with the provisions of the Act of Congress above quoted, and it is so ordered.

Tams Bixby    Commissioner.

Muskogee, Indian Territory.
MAR 14 1906

---

7-4737

Muskogee, Indian Territory, May 18, 1904.

Jimmie Nail,
South McAlester, Indian Territory.

Dear Sir:

Receipt is hereby acknowledged of the affidavits of Beckie Nail and Nancy Cable, relative to the birth of your infant son, Dick Nail, March 27, 1902.

# Applications for Enrollment of Choctaw Newborn
## Act of 1905  Volume XX

You are informed that although said child was born prior to the ratification on September 25, 1902, of The Act of Congress approved July 1, 1902, it does not appear from our records that any previous application has ever been made for his enrollment, and under the provisions of said Act of Congress, the Commission is now without authority to receive or consider the original application for enrollment of any person whomsoever as a citizen of the Choctaw or Chickasaw Nation.

Respectfully,

Commissioner in Charge.

_____

Choctaw 4737.

Muskogee, Indian Territory, March 31, 1905.

Jimmie Nail,
Blanco, Indian Territory.

Dear Sir:

Receipt is hereby acknowledged of the affidavits of Beckie Nail and Martha E. Dailey to the birth of Dock Nail, son of Jimmie and Beckie Nail, March 4th, 1902, and the same have been filed with our records as an application for the enrollment of said child.

Respectfully,

Chairman.

_____

7-4737.

Muskogee, Indian Territory, May 5, 1905.

Jimmie Nail,
Blanco, Indian Territory.

Dear Sir:

Receipt is hereby acknowledged of your affidavit which is offered in support of the application for the enrollment of your child, Doctor Nail, and the same has been filed with the records in this case.

Respectfully,

Commissioner in Charge.

_____

7-4737

Muskogee, Indian Territory, August 4, 1905.

Wallace Wilkinson,
    Attorney at Law.
        South McAlester, Indian Territory.

Dear Sir:

Receipt is hereby acknowledged of your letter of July 29, 1905, asking if Dock Nail, child of Jimmie Nail has been enrolled.

In reply to your letter you are advised that the name of Dock Nail has not yet been placed upon a schedule of citizens by blood of the Choctaw Nation prepared for forwarding to the Secretary of the Interior, but if additional evidence is necessary in this case you will be notified.

Respectfully,

Commissioner.

---

7-4737.

Muskogee, Indian Territory, September 8, 1905.

Wallace Wilkinson,
    Attorney at Law,
        South McAlester, Indian Territory.

Dear Sir:

In the matter of the application for the enrollment of Dock Nail, minor son of Jimmie Nail and Becky Nail, as a citizen by blood of the Choctaw Nation there are on file a number of affidavits as to the birth of said child in which the date of his birth is variously stated as March 27, 1902, March 27, 1903 and March 4, 1902.

It will be necessary, before the rights of said child can be finally determined, that this office be supplied with the joint affidavit of the parents of said child stating which of the above dates, if either of them, is the correct date of the birth of said child.

There is also on file with the record in this case marriage license and certificate showing marriage between James Nail and Mrs. Jane Tucker. It will be necessary for you to furnish this office with evidence tending to show whether or not the said Jane Tucker mentioned in said marriage license and certificate is identical with Becky Nail or Beckie Nail, the mother of said Dock Nail.

Respectfully,

Acting Commissioner.

---

7 - 4737-

Muskogee, Indian Territory, October 19, 1905.

Jimmie Nail,
    Blanco, Indian Territory.

Dear Sir:

In the matter of the application for the enrollment of your minor son, Dock Nail, as a citizen by blood of the Choctaw Nation, there are on file a number of affidavits as to the birth of said child in which the date of his birth is variously stated as March 27, 1902, March 27, 1903 and March 4, 1902. It will be necessary, before the rights of said child can be finally determined, that this office be supplied with the joint affidavit of the parents of said child stating which of the above dates, if either of them, is the correct date of the birth of said child.

There is also on file with the record in this case marriage license and certificate showing marriage between James Nail and Mrs. Jane Tucker. It will be necessary for you to furnish this office with evidence tending to show whether or not the said Jane Tucker mentioned in said marriage license and certificate is identical with Becky Nail or Beckie Nail, the mother of said Dock Nail.

Respectfully,

Commissioner.

---

7-4737.

Muskogee, Indian Territory, October 19, 1905.

McCurtain & Hill,
    Attorneys at Law,
        South McAlester, Indian Territory.

Gentlemen:

In the matter of the application for the enrollment of Dock Nail, minor son of Jimmie Nail and Becky Nail, as a citizen by blood of the Choctaw Nation there are on file a number of affidavits as to the birth of said child in which the date of his birth is variously stated as March 27, 1902, March 27, 1903 and March 4, 1902.

# Applications for Enrollment of Choctaw Newborn
## Act of 1905   Volume XX

It will be necessary, before the rights of said child can be finally determined, that this office be supplied with the joint affidavit of the parents of said child stating which of the above dates, if either of them, is the correct date of the birth of said child.

There is also on file with the record in this case marriage license and certificate showing marriage between James Nail and Mrs. Jane Tucker.  It will be necessary for you to furnish this office with evidence tending to show whether or not the said Jane Tucker mentioned in said marriage license and certificate is identical with Becky Nail or Beckie Nail, the mother of said Dock Nail.

Respectfully,

Commissioner.

---

7-4737.

Muskogee, Indian Territory, January 2, 1906.

Wallace Wilkinson,
>   Attorney at Law,
>>      South McAlester, Indian Territory.

Dear Sir:

Receipt is hereby acknowledged of your letter of December 2, 1905, inclosing joint affidavit of Jimmie Nail and Becky Jane Nail which you offer in support of the application for the enrollment of Dock Nail and the same has been filed in the matter of the enrollment of said child.

Respectfully,

Commissioner.

---

7-NB-1520

Muskogee, Indian Territory, March 14, 1906.

Jimmie Nail,
>   Blanco, Indian Territory.

Dear Sir:

Inclosed herewith you will find a copy of the decision of the Commissioner to the Five Civilized Tribes, rendered March 14, 1906, granting the application for the enrollment of your minor child, Dock Nail, as a citizen by blood of the Choctaw Nation.

143

The attorneys for the Choctaw and Chickasaw Nation[sic] have been furnished a copy of this decision and have been allowed fifteen days from the date of this notice within which to file protest against his enrollment. If at the expiration of that time no protest has been filed, the name of Dock Nail will be placed upon the final roll of citizens by blood of the Choctaw Nation to be submitted to the Secretary of the Interior for his approval.

Respectfully,

Signed   Wm. O. Beall

Registered.                                         Acting Commissioner.

Incl. 7-NB-1520.

---

7-NB-1520.

Muskogee, Indian Territory, March 14, 1906.

**COPY**

Presley B. Cole,
>   Attorney at Law,
>>      South McAlester, Indian Territory.

Dear Sir:

You are hereby notified that the Commissioner to the Five Civilized Tribes, on March 14, 1906, rendered his decision granting the application for the enrollment of Dock Nail as a citizen by blood of the Choctaw Nation.

The attorneys for the Choctaw and Chickasaw Nations have been furnished a copy of this decision and have been allowed fifteen days from the date of this notice within which to file protest against his enrollment. If at the expiration of that time no protest has been filed, the name of Dock Nail will be placed upon the final roll of citizens by blood of the Choctaw Nation to be submitted to the Secretary of the Interior for his approval.

Respectfully,

Signed

Wm. O. Beall

Registered.                                         Acting Commissioner.

---

7-NB-1520.

Muskogee, Indian Territory, March 14, 1906.
**COPY**

Mansfield, McMurray & Cornish,
    Attorneys for Choctaw and Chickasaw Nations,
        South McAlester, Indian Territory.

Gentlemen:

Inclosed herewith you will find a copy of the decision of the Commissioner to the Five Civilized Tribes, rendered March 14, 1906, granting the application for the enrollment of Dock Nail as a citizen by blood of the Choctaw Nation.

You are hereby advised that you will be allowed fifteen days from the date of this notice within which to file protest against his enrollment. If at the expiration of that time no protest has been filed, the name of Dock Nail will be placed upon the final roll of citizens by blood of the Choctaw Nation to be submitted to the Secretary of the Interior for his approval.

Respectfully,

Signed
*Wm. O. Beall*

Registered.
Incl. 7-NB-1520.

Acting Commissioner.

---

7-NB-1520

Muskogee, Indian Territory, August 23, 1906.

James Nail,
    Blanco, Indian Territory.

Dear Sir:-

Receipt is hereby acknowledged of your letter of July 25, 1906, asking the status of the application for the enrollment of your child, Doc Nail, now three years of age.

In reply you are advised that the name of your child, Dock Nail, has been placed upon a schedule of new born citizens of the Choctaw Nation, under the Act of Congress approved March 3, 1905, which has been forwarded to the Secretary of the Interior, but this office has not been notified of Departmental action thereon. You will be advised when his enrollment has been approved by the Department.

Respectfully,

Commissioner.

Choc. New Born 1521
>  Rebecca Elsie Cooper
>  (Born Jan. 31, 1906)

1521

## NEW BORN
### CHOCTAW
### ENROLLMENT

REBECCA ELSIE COOPER

(BORN JANUARY 31, 1906)

As Citizen of the
CHOCTAW NATION
Act of Congress
Approved March 3, 1905

C A N C E L L E D

RECORD TRANSFERRED TO CHOCTAW NEW BORN
#789
ACT OF CONGRESS APPROVED APRIL 26, 1906.
JULY 20, 1906

1521

## CHOCTAW     1521
### NEW BORN
ACT OF CONGRESS APPROVED MARCH 30, 1905.

*Rebecca Elsie Cooper*
*(Born January 31, 1906)*

# CANCELLED

*Record transferred to*
*Choctaw New Born 789*
ACT OF CONGRESS APPROVED APRIL 26, 1906.
**JUL 20 1906**

Choc. New Born 1522
>   Jackson Baker, Jr.
>   (Born Nov. 6, 1905)

1522

# NEW BORN
## CHOCTAW
### ENROLLMENT

JACKSON BAKER, JR.

(BORN NOVEMBER 6, 1905)

As Citizen of the
CHOCTAW NATION
Act of Congress
Approved March 3, 1905

C A N C E L L E D

TRANSFERRED TO CHOCTAW NEW BORN NO. 765
ACT OF CONGRESS APPROVED APRIL 26, 1906.

AUGUST 17, 1906

1522

# CHOCTAW       1522

# NEW BORN
ACT OF CONGRESS APPROVED MARCH 30, 1905.

*Jackson Baker, Jr.*
*(Born Nov. 6, 1905)*

# CANCELLED

*Transferred to* CHOCTAW

NEW BORN *No 765.*

ACT OF CONGRESS APPROVED APRIL 26, 1906.
**AUG 17 1906**

Choc. New Born 1523
  Wiley Paddock
  (Born Aug. 24, 1905)

———————

**1523**

## NEW BORN
### CHOCTAW
### ENROLLMENT

WILEY PADDOCK

(BORN AUGUST 24, 1905)
As Citizen of the
CHOCTAW NATION
Act of Congress
Approved March 3, 1905

C A N C E L L E D

RECORD TRANSFERRED to CHOCTAW N. B. NO. 496
ACT OF CONGRESS APPROVED APRIL 26, 1906.

JULY 13, 1906

**1523**

———————

# CHOCTAW          1523

# NEW BORN
ACT OF CONGRESS APPROVED MARCH 30, 1905.

*Wiley Paddock*
*(Born)*
*(August 24, 1905)*

# CANCELLED
*Record transferred to*
*Choctaw New Born #496*
ACT OF CONGRESS APPROVED APRIL 26, 1906.
**JUL 13 1906**

<u>Choc. New Born 1524</u>
Ruth Gould
(Born Aug. 23, 1905)

———————

1524

# NEW BORN
## CHOCTAW
### ENROLLMENT

RUTH GOULD

(BORN AUGUST 23, 1905)

As Citizen of the
CHOCTAW NATION
Act of Congress
Approved March 3, 1905

CANCELLED

RECORD TRANSFERRED TO CHOCTAW
NEW BORN NO. 819.

ACT OF CONGRESS APPROVED APRIL 26, 1906.
JULY 20, 1906

1524

———————

# CHOCTAW        1524

# NEW BORN
ACT OF CONGRESS APPROVED MARCH 30, 1905.

*Ruth Gould*
*(Born Aug 23, 1905)*

# CANCELLED

*Record transferred to*
*Choctaw New Born 819*
ACT OF CONGRESS APPROVED APRIL 26, 1906.

**JUL 20 1906**

<u>Choc. New Born 1525</u>
>Jesse Johnson Town
>(Born July 22, 1904)

1525

# NEW BORN
## CHOCTAW
### ENROLLMENT

JESSE JOHNSON TOWN

(BORN JULY 22, 1904)

As Citizen of the
CHOCTAW NATION
Act of Congress
Approved March 3, 1905

TRANSFERRED TO CHOCTAW N.B. (APRIL 26, 1906) #1289

**1525**

*Cho*   (Corner torn off)

*Jesse Johnson Town*
*(July 22 1904)*

*Transferred to Choc N. B.*
*(Apr. 26, 06) #1289*

<u>Choc. New Born 1526</u>
>Wilson Fisher
>(Born Apr. 27, 1905)

1526

## NEW BORN
CHOCTAW
ENROLLMENT

WILSON FISHER

(BORN APRIL 27, 1905)

As Citizen of the
CHOCTAW NATION
Act of Congress
Approved March 3, 1905

C A N C E L L E D

RECORD TRANSFERRED TO CHOCTAW NEW BORN
#627

ACT OF CONGRESS APPROVED APRIL 26, 1906.
JULY 13, 1906

1526

---

# CHOCTAW      1526

## NEW BORN
ACT OF CONGRESS APPROVED MARCH 30, 1905.

*Wilson Fisher*
*(Born April 27, 1905)*

# CANCELLED

*Record transferred to*
*Choctaw New Born #637*
ACT OF CONGRESS APPROVED APRIL 26, 1906.

**JUL 13 1906**

Choc. New Born 1527
　　　Everett Vaunto Jones
　　　(Born June 28, 1905)

---

1527

## NEW BORN
### CHOCTAW
### ENROLLMENT

EVERETT VAUNTO JONES.

(BORN JUNE 28, 1905)

As Citizen of the
CHOCTAW NATION
Act of Congress
Approved March 3, 1905

C A N C E L L E D

TRANSFERRED TO CHOCTAW NEW BORN NO. 333
ACT OF CONGRESS APPROVED APRIL 26, 1906.
AUGUST 17, 1906

1527

---

# CHOCTAW          1527
# NEW BORN
ACT OF CONGRESS APPROVED MARCH 30, 1905.

*Everett Vaunto Jones*
*(Born June 28, 1905)*

# CANCELLED

*transferred to* CHOCTAW
NEW BORN *No 333*
ACT OF CONGRESS APPROVED APRIL 26, 1906.
**AUG 17 1906**

Choc. New Born 1528
    William Sunny
    (Born Oct. 6, 1903)

1528

# NEW BORN
## CHOCTAW
### ENROLLMENT

### WILLIAM SUNNY

(BORN OCTOBER 6, 1903)

As Citizen of the
## CHOCTAW NATION
Act of Congress
Approved March 3, 1905

DISMISSED

MAY 4, 1906

## 1528

7-1627

Muskogee, Indian Territory, March 15, 1905.

James Sunny,
    Sawyer, Indian Territory.

Dear Sir:

Receipt is hereby acknowledged of the affidavits of Fannie Sunny, James Sunny and John Ahikatubby[sic] Reed to the birth of William Sunny, infant child of James and Fannie Sunny, October 6, 1903, and the affidavit of Sallie Evans that said child lived about three hours.

You are advised that by the act of Congress approved March 3, 1905, the Commission is authorized to receive applications for the enrollment of children born to recognized and enrolled citizens of the Choctaw Nation subsequent to September 25, 1902, and prior to March 4, 1905, and living on the latter date.  You will therefore see that the Commission is without authority to enroll children born subsequent to September 25, 1902, who were not living on March 4, 1905.

Respectfully,

Chairman.

---

7-NB-1528

Muskogee, Indian Territory, May 4, 1906.

James Sunny,
    Sawyer, Indian Territory.

Dear Sir:

You are hereby advised that it appearing from the records of this office that your infant child, William Sunny died prior to March 4, 1905, the Commissioner to the Five Civilized Tribes, on May 4, 1906, dismissed the application for his enrollment as a citizen by blood of the Choctaw Nation.

Respectfully,

Wm. O. Beall

Acting Commissioner.

---

Indian Territory.
Central Judicial Division } SS

On this 16th day of January, A.D. 1905, personally appeared before me a Notary Public of the above Judicial District, Mrs. Sallie Evans and after being sworn by me deposes and says that she was present and assisted ~~Dr. E. R. Baker~~ in an obstetrical case when Mrs. James Sunny was confined - on the 6th day of October 1903, where a son William was born to the above James Sunny and wife Fannie Sunny, and that he was living and Christened and continued to live about 3 hours. Also that Mrs. H.C. Coleman (illegible) was also present.

Witness my hand and seal this day and year (illegible) above named

Mrs. Sallie Evans　　[Seal]

*Sworn to and subscribed before me this 10th day of January A.D. 1905*
*Ale Davis Notary Public*
*Central Judicial Division*
*Indian Territory*

*My com expires April 25 1907.*

**NEW-BORN AFFIDAVIT.**

Number...................

# Choctaw Enrolling Commission.

IN THE MATTER OF THE APPLICATION FOR ENROLLMENT, as a citizen of the
Choctaw    Nation, of                    William Sunny

born on the    6th   day of    October      190 3

Name of father    James Sunny                    a citizen of    Choctaw
Nation final enrollment No    4604
Name of mother    Fannie Sunny                   a citizen of   White intermarried
Nation final enrollment No ——

Postoffice    Sawyer IT

**AFFIDAVIT OF MOTHER.**

UNITED STATES OF AMERICA, ⎫
   INDIAN TERRITORY, ⎬
  Central      DISTRICT ⎭

    I              Fannie Sunny                    on oath state that I
am   22   years of age and a citizen by   intemiage[sic]      of the   Choctaw      Nation,
and as such have been placed upon the final roll of the    ———    Nation, by the Honorable
Secretary of the Interior my final enrollment number being  ——   ; that I am the lawful wife
of    James Sunny              , who is a citizen of the    Choctaw        Nation, and as such
has been placed upon the final roll of said Nation by the Honorable Secretary of the Interior,
his final enrollment number being   4604    and that a    male    child was born to me on the
6th    day of    October    190 3 ; that said child has been named    William Sunny       ,
and is now living.

                    Fannie Sunny

WITNESSETH:
  Must be two  ⎫  Moses Roberts
  Witnesses who ⎬
  are Citizens.  ⎭  Daniel Roberts

## Applications for Enrollment of Choctaw Newborn
## Act of 1905   Volume XX

Subscribed and sworn to before me this     18     day of     Jan          190 5

W A Shoney
Notary Public.

My commission expires     Jan 10 1909

---

It appearing from the within affidavits that William Sunny, born October 6, 1903, for whose enrollment as a citizen by blood of the Choctaw Nation, application was made under the Act of Congress approved March 3, 1905, (33 Stats., 1071), died October 6, 1903, it is hereby ordered that the application for the enrollment of said William Sunny as a citizen by blood of the Choctaw Nation be dismissed.

Tams Bixby   Commissioner.

Muskogee, Indian Territory.
MAY 4 – 1906

---

DEATH AFFIDAVIT

NO._____

# Choctaw Enrolling Commission.

IN THE MATTER OF THE DEATH OF                    William Sunny

a citizen of the     Choctaw          Nation, who formerly resided at or near     Sawyer
Ind. Ter., and died on the   same day birth 6th          day of     Oct          190 3

## AFFIDAVIT OF RELATIVE.

UNITED STATES OF AMERICA
INDIAN TERRITORY
    Central          DISTRICT.

I,    James Sunny               on oath, state that I am   35       years of age, and a citizen of the     Choctaw          Nation, and as such have been finally enrolled by the Honorable Secretary of the Interior, my enrollment number being    4604          ; that my postoffice address is    Sawyer     , Ind. Ter.; that I am   the father     of    the child     who was a citizen, by blood   , of the    Choctaw     Nation; and that said   William Sunny     died on the     6th day of   Oct     , 190 3

WITNESSETH:

Must be two  { M.W. Battice
witnesses who {                                         James Sunny
are Citizens.  { _____

156

Subscribed and sworn to before me this the    18<sup>th</sup>       day of
Jan          190  5

W A Shoney          Notary Public.

## AFFIDAVIT OF ACQUAINTANCE.

UNITED STATES OF AMERICA
INDIAN TERRITORY
Central        DISTRICT.


I,     John Reed              on oath, state that I am     28      years of age, and a
citizen by    blood       of the     Choctaw            Nation; that my post-office address is
Sawyer            Ind. Ter.; that I was personally acquainted with    William Sunny          the
deceased child above named, who was a citizen of     Choctaw           Nation by blood, and that
said    William Sunny       died on the    6<sup>th</sup>     day of     Oct    , 190 3

John Ahekatubby Reed

Subscribed and sworn to before me this    19      day of    January        190 5

Ale Davis          Notary Public.

My Commission Expires:    April 25, 1907

---

Choc. New Born 1529
        Jewell Mary Beal
        (Born Jan. 1, 1904)

**1529**

# NEW BORN
## CHOCTAW
### ENROLLMENT

JEWELL MARY BEAL

(BORN JANUARY 1, 1904)

As Citizen of the
CHOCTAW NATION
Act of Congress
Approved March 3, 1905

NO ............HEREON DISMISSED UNDER ORDER OF
THE COMMISSIONER TO THE FIVE CIVILIZED
TRIBES OF JULY 18, 1905.

JUNE 26, 1906

NOTICE OF DECISION FORWARDED
APPLICANT'S FATHER JUNE 26, 1906

## 1529

# Department of the Interior,
### COMMISSION TO THE FIVE CIVILIZED TRIBES.

*IN RE Application for Enrollment,* as a citizen of the　　　Choctaw　　　Nation,
of　　　Jewell Mary Beal　　　, born on the　1$^{st}$　day of　January　, 1904

Name of Father: Reuben Beal Jr.　　　　　　a citizen of the　Choctaw　　Nation.
Name of Mother: Mosie Beal　　　　　　　a citizen of the　U. S.　　~~Nation.~~

Post-Office:　　Silo, I. T.

**AFFIDAVIT OF MOTHER.**

UNITED STATES OF AMERICA,
　INDIAN TERRITORY
　　Western　　　　　District.

　　I,　Mosie Beal　　, on oath, state that I am　19　years of age and a citizen, by
marriage　, of the　Choctaw　Nation; that I am the lawful wife of　Reuben Beal Jr.　,
who is a citizen, by　blood　of the Choctaw　Nation; that a　girl　child was born
to me on　the 1$^{st}$　day of　January , 1904; that said child has been named　Jewell
Mary Beal　, and is now living.

Mosie Beal

Subscribed and sworn to before me this　6$^{th}$　day of　March　, 1905.

JB Campbell
Notary Public.

# Applications for Enrollment of Choctaw Newborn
## Act of 1905   Volume XX

### AFFIDAVIT OF ATTENDING PHYSICIAN, OR MID-WIFE.

UNITED STATES OF AMERICA,
INDIAN TERRITORY

Central          District.

I,   B. Gardner          , a     midwife     , on oath, state that I attended on Mrs.   Mosie Beal    , wife of    Reuben Beal Jr    on the    1$^{st}$    day of January    , 1904 ; that there was born to her on said date a    female    child; that said child is now ~~living~~ *deceased* and is said to have been named    Jewell Mary Beal

B. Gardner
*midwife*

Subscribed and sworn to before me this   8$^{th}$   day of    March   , 1904.

W.H. Ritchey
Notary Public.

---

It appearing from the within affidavits that Jewell Mary Beal, born January 1, 1904, for whose enrollment as a citizen by blood of the Choctaw Nation, application made under the Act of Congress approved March 3, 1905, (33 Stat., 1071), died August 11, 1904, it is hereby ordered that the application for the enrollment of said Jewell Mary Beal as a citizen by blood of the Choctaw Nation, be dismissed.

Tams Bixby    Commissioner.

Muskogee, Indian Territory,
JUN 26 1906

---

DEATH AFFIDAVIT

NO._____

## Choctaw Enrolling Commission.

IN THE MATTER OF THE DEATH OF      Jewel Mary Beal
a citizen of the    Choctaw    Nation, who formerly resided at or near    Durant
Ind. Ter., and died on the    11$^{th}$      day of    August      190 4

# Applications for Enrollment of Choctaw Newborn
## Act of 1905   Volume XX

## AFFIDAVIT OF RELATIVE.

UNITED STATES OF AMERICA
INDIAN TERRITORY
Central        DISTRICT.

I,     Reuben Beal Jr             on oath, state that I am     26     years of age, and a citizen of the        Choctaw             Nation, and as such have been finally enrolled by the Honorable Secretary of the Interior, my enrollment number being      15725              ; that my postoffice address is      Silo     , Ind. Ter.; that I am    the father     of     Jewel Mary Beal who was a citizen, by     Blood    , of the     Choctaw     Nation; and that said     Jewel Mary Beal died on the    11<sup>th</sup>      day of     August    , 190  4

WITNESSETH:

Must be two
witnesses who
are Citizens.

(Name Illegible)

B. Gardner

Reuben Beal Jr

Subscribed and sworn to before me this the      8<sup>th</sup>      day of
March              190 5

W.H. Ritchey     Notary Public.

## AFFIDAVIT OF ACQUAINTANCE.

UNITED STATES OF AMERICA
INDIAN TERRITORY
Central        DISTRICT.

I,     W A Durant             on oath, state that I am     38     years of age, and a citizen by     Blood     of the     Choctaw     Nation; that my post-office address is Durant        Ind. Ter.; that I was personally acquainted with     Jewel Mary Beal       the deceased child above named, who was a citizen of     Choctaw     Nation by blood, and that said    Jewel Mary Beal      died on the    11     day of     August    , 190 4

W A Durant

Subscribed and sworn to before me this     8     day of    March        190

W.H. Ritchey     Notary Public.

My Commission Expires:

7-5845

Muskogee, Indian Territory, March 13, 1905.

Reuben Beal,
    Silo, Indian Territory.

Dear Sir:

    Receipt is hereby acknowledged of the affidavits of Mosie Beal and B. Gardner to the birth of Jewell Mary Beal, daughter of Reuben Beal, Jr., and Mosie Beal, January 1, 1904, and the affidavits of Reuben Beal, Jr., and W. A. Durant to the death of said child August 11, 1904.

    You are advised that under the provisions of the act of Congress approved March 3, 1905, the Commission is authorized for sixty days from that date to receive only the applications for the enrollment of infant children born subsequent to September 25, 1902, and prior to March 4, 1905, who were living on the latter date.  The Commission is therefore without authority to enroll children born subsequent to September 25, 1902, who have died prior to March 4, 1905.

Respectfully,

Chairman.

---

7-1529

**COPY**

Muskogee, Indian Territory, June 26, 1906.

Reuben Beal, Jr.,
    Silo, Indian Territory.

Dear Sir:

    You are hereby advised that it appearing from the records of this office that your child, Jewell Mary Beal, died prior to March 4, 1906, the Commissioner to the Five Civilized Tribes on June 26, 1906, dismissed the application for her enrollment as a citizen by blood of the Choctaw Nation.

Respectfully,

SIGNED    *Tams Bixby*
Commissioner.

Choc. New Born 1530
   Belinda Wade
   (Born May 10, 1904)

---

**NEW BORN**

*JCS*

*Belinda Wade*

*Choctaw Nation*

*Approved* **JAN 19 1907**

*Tams Bixby*

*Commissioner.*

*Born May 10, 1904*

ACT OF CONGRESS APPROVED MARCH 30, 1905.

**JUL 5- 1906**

CHOCTAW                    **APR 21 1905**

*NB 1530*

---

Birth Affidavit.

## DEPARTMENT OF THE INTERIOR,
## COMMISSION TO THE FIVE CIVILIZED TRIBES.

---

IN RE APPLICATION FOR ENROLLMENT, as a citizen of the      Choctaw      Nation,
of      Belinda Wade          , born on the      10      day of      May      1904

Name of Father:   Ben Wade                    a citizen of the   Choctaw   Nation.
Name of Mother:   Mimie Wade                  a citizen of the   Choctaw   Nation.

Post Office      Lukfata I.T.

---

## AFFIDAVIT OF MOTHER.

United States of America,    |
Indian Territory,            | ss.
   Central         District. |

   I,   Mimie Wade     , on oath state that I am   20   years of age and a citizen by
Blood    , of the   Choctaw   Nation; that I am lawful wife of      Ben Wade          ,
who is a citizen, by     Blood   of the   Choctaw   Nation; that a     Female     child was

born to me on   10<sup>th</sup>   day of   May   1904  that said child has been named   Belinda
Wade   , and was living March 4, 1905.

Mimie Wade

WITNESS TO MARK:
  Louis Anderson
  Simon Going


  Subscribed and sworn to before me this   17  day of   April   1905.


W.P. Wilson<br>Notary Public.

---

AFFIDAVIT OF ATTENDING PHYSICIAN OR MIDWIFE.

United States of America,   |
Indian Territory,            | ss.
  Central   District.        |

  I,   Louisa Anderson   , a   Midwife   , on oath state that I attended on
Mrs.   Mimie Wade   , wife of   Ben   on the   10<sup>th</sup>   day of   May   1904
that there was born to her on said date a   Female   child; that said child was living
March 4, 1905, and is said to have been named   ~~Louisa Anderson~~  Belinda Wade

Louisa Anderson

WITNESSES TO MARK:
  Louis Anderson
  Simon Going


  Subscribed and sworn to before me this   17  day of   April   1905.


W.P. Wilson<br>NOTARY PUBLIC.

---

Muskogee, Indian Territory, April 24, 1905.

Ben Wade,
    Lukfata, Indian Territory.

Dear Sir:

    Receipt is hereby acknowledged of the affidavits of Minnie[sic] Wade and Louisa
Anderson to the birth of Belinda Wade, daughter of Ben and Minnie Wade, May 10,
1904.

# Applications for Enrollment of Choctaw Newborn
## Act of 1905  Volume XX

It is stated in the affidavit of the mother that she is a citizen by blood of the Choctaw Nation. If this is correct you are requested to state the name under which she was enrolled, the names of her parents, and if she has selected an allotment of the lands of the Choctaw or Chickasaw Nation please give her roll number as it appears upon her allotment certificate.

Respectfully,

Chairman.

---

Muskogee, Indian Territory, May 29, 1905.

Ben Wade,
 Lukfata, Indian Territory.

Dear Sir:

Referring to the application for the enrollment of your child, Belinda Wade, a letter was addressed to you on April 24, asking information which yould[sic] enable us to identify the mother of this child upon our records.

Before further consideration can be given this application it will be necessary that you give the name under which your wife, Mimie Wade, was enrolled, the names of her parents and if she has selected an allotment of the lands of the Choctaw or Chickasaw Nation, give her roll number as it appears upon her allotment certificate.

This matter should receive immediate attention.

Respectfully,

Chairman.

---

7-NB-1530

Muskogee, Indian Territory, September 14, 1906.

Ben Wade,
 Lukfata, Indian Territory.

Dear Sir:

In the matter of the application for the enrollment of your child Belinda Wade under the act of Congress approved March 3, 1905, you are advised that this matter is now receiving consideration and in event additional evidence is necessary to enable this office to determine the right to enrollment of this child you will be duly notified.

164

Respectfully,

Commissioner.

23-1530

Muskogee, Indian Territory, March 8, 1907.

Chief Clerk,
    Choctaw Land Office,
        Atoka, Indian Territory.

Dear Sir:

In compliance with your request of February 27, 1907, there is inclosed you herewith copy of Choctaw New Born roll card 1530, and you are directed to make duplicate card of this number in your possession conform to the information thereon.

Respectfully,

EB 1-9.

Commissioner.

---

Choc. New Born 1531
    Kitsie Lewis
    *(Birthdate not given.)*

**1531**

# NEW BORN
## CHOCTAW
### ENROLLMENT

KITSIE LEWIS

As Citizen of the
CHOCTAW NATION
Act of Congress
Approved March 3, 1905

TRANSFERRED TO 7-479
FEBRUARY 19, 1907

G R A N T E D

## 1531

---

*1531*

*Choctaw*   NEW BORN
*(Act March 3 1905)*

*Kitsie Lewis*
*Transferred to 7-479*
*Feb 19 - 1907*
*Granted*

---

Choc. New Born 1532
    Sally Thomas
    *(January 3, 1904)*

---

1532

# NEW BORN
## CHOCTAW
### ENROLLMENT

SALLY THOMAS

As Citizen of the
CHOCTAW NATION
Act of Congress
Approved March 3, 1905

DISMISSED FEBRUARY 1, 1907

## 1532

---

# Applications for Enrollment of Choctaw Newborn
## Act of 1905   Volume XX

BIRTH AFFIDAVIT.

### DEPARTMENT OF THE INTERIOR,
## COMMISSIONER TO THE FIVE CIVILIZED TRIBES.

ENROLLMENT OF MINORS.   ACT OF CONGRESS, APPROVED APRIL 26, 1906.

IN RE APPLICATION FOR ENROLLMENT, as a citizen of the      Choctaw      Nation,

of    Sally Thomas               , born on the   3   day of   January  , 1904

Name of Father:  Benson Thomas                a citizen of the   Choctaw      Nation.
Name of Mother:  Ida Thomas                   a citizen of the   Choctaw      Nation.

Tribal enrollment of father ............................ Tribal enrollment of mother ...........................

Postoffice      Soper, Indian Territory

---

AFFIDAVIT OF MOTHER.

UNITED STATES OF AMERICA, Indian Territory,
Central                       District.

I,      Ida Thomas               , on oath state that I am   22     years of age
and a citizen by      blood      , of the      Choctaw      Nation; that I am the lawful
wife of   Benson Thomas      , who is a citizen, by      blood      of the      Choctaw
Nation; that a   Female   child was born to me on   3rd   day of   January  , 1904 , that
said child has been named     Sally Thomas     , and was living ~~March 4, 1906~~.

her<br>
Ida (x) Thomas<br>
mark

WITNESSES TO MARK:
{ J O Nail
{ Carl Patterson

Subscribed and sworn to before me this  26   day of   January  , 190 7.

Carl Patterson
Notary Public.

---

AFFIDAVIT OF ATTENDING PHYSICIAN OR MID-WIFE.

UNITED STATES OF AMERICA, Indian Territory,
Central                       District.

I,      Sweney Wallace      , a      mid-wife         , on oath state that I
attended on   Ida Thomas   , wife of     Benson Thomas    on the 3rd day of   January ,
1904 ; that there was born to her on said date a   Female   child; that said child was living
March 4, 1906, and is said to have been named  Sally Thomas

# Applications for Enrollment of Choctaw Newborn
## Act of 1905   Volume XX

Sweney Wallace

{

Subscribed and sworn to before me this 26th   day of   January  , 190 7.

Carl Patterson
Notary Public.

---

It appearing from the within affidavits that Sally Thomas for whose enrollment application was made under the Act of Congress approved March 3, 1905 (33 Stat., 1060), died prior to March 4, 1905, I am of the opinion that the application for her enrollment as a new born citizen of the Choctaw Nation should be dismissed and it is so ordered.

Tams Bixby   Commissioner.

Muskogee, Indian Territory.

---

## Department of the Interior.
## COMMISSIONER TO THE FIVE CIVILIZED TRIBES.

*In the matter of the death of*          Sally Thomas

a citizen of the      Choctaw      Nation, who formerly resided at or near      Soper      ,
Ind. Ter., and died on the      24th      day of    January      , 1905

---

### AFFIDAVIT OF RELATIVE.

Central District   }

I,    Benson Thomas      , on oath state that I am    34    years of age and a citizen by    blood   , of the   Choctaw   Nation; that my postoffice address is    Soper      , Ind. Ter.; that I am    the father    of    Sally Thomas      who was a citizen, by    blood   , of the    Choctaw      Nation and that said    Sally Thomas      died on the    24      day of January    , 1905

Benson Thomas

{

Subscribed and sworn to before me this    26th      day of    January      , 190 7.

Carl Patterson
Notary Public.

168

# Applications for Enrollment of Choctaw Newborn
## Act of 1905   Volume XX

Central District }

I,    J.O. Nail    , on oath state that I am    36    years of age, and a citizen by blood   of the    Choctaw    Nation; that my postoffice address is    Soper    , Ind. Ter.; that I was personally acquainted with    Sally Thomas    who was a citizen, by    blood  , of the    Choctaw    Nation; and that said    Sally Thomas    died on the    24    day of January    , 1905

J O Nail

WITNESSES TO MARK:

{

Subscribed and sworn to before me this    26th    day of    January    , 1907.

Carl Patterson
Notary Public.

---

## DEPARTMENT OF THE INTERIOR.
## COMMISSIONER TO THE FIVE CIVILIZED TRIBES.

Soper, Indian Territory, February 11, 1907.

In the matter of the application for the enrollment of (Sallie) Thomas, deceased child of Benson Thomas and Ida Thomas, as a citizen of the Choctaw Nation, under the Act of Congress approved March 3, 1905.

Benson Thomas, being first duly sworn and examined, testifies as follows:

ON BEHALF OF THE COMMISSIONER:

Q What is your name? A Benson Thomas.
Q How old are you? A About thirty-four.
Q What is your postoffice address? A Soper.
Q What is the name of your father? A Johnson Thomas.
Q What was the name of your mother? A Natsy.
Q What is the name of your wife? A Ida Thomas, but she is enrolled as Ida Ward.
Q Have you had any children by your wife, Ida? A Yes, sir.
Q What was this child's name? A Sallie.
Q When was Sallie Born? A January 3, 1904.
Q Is Sallie still living? A No, she died.
Q When did she die? A January 24, 1905.
Q This is the only child you have had by your wife, Ida, is it? A Yes, sir.

169

# Applications for Enrollment of Choctaw Newborn
## Act of 1905   Volume XX

Q And this child, Sallie Thomas died on January 24, 1905, did she? A Yes, sir.

Q Have you received a letter from the Commissioner relative to the enrollment of this child, Sallie? A Yes, sir, I got one last Saturday and they said they couldn't enroll it, because it died too soon.

Q Have you made an affidavit relative to the death of this child? A Yes, sir, about two weeks ago.

Q Who got this affidavit? A One of the Commissioners.

Q Do you know his name? A Yes, sir, it was Mr. Patterson.

Q He got an affidavit relative to the death of this child, did he? A Yes, sir.

(Witness excused)

I, Fay E. Blachert, stenographer to the Commissioner to the Five Civilized Tribes, upon oath, state that I reported the proceedings in the above and foregoing cause, and that the same is a true and correct transcript of my stenographic notes taken therein.

Fay E. Blachert

Subscribed and sworn to before me this 11th day of February, 1907.

Richard Shanafelt
Notary Public.

---

*May The 2ᵈ 1905*

*To The Commission to the five civilized tribes in case there has not been an application made for the enrollment of the infant child of Benson Thomas and Ida Thomas I hereby make an application for said child to be enrolled as a citizen by blood of the Choctaw Nation*

*G. J. Humphreys*
*Ardmore, I T*

---

# Applications for Enrollment of Choctaw Newborn
## Act of 1905   Volume XX

Soper I. T.  January 26, 1907.

Commissioner 5 Civilized Tribes,
Muskogee, I. T.

Dear Sir:-

Youn[sic] will find enclosed herewith new affidavits relative to the birth of Sally Thomas who is an applicant for enrollment as a Choctaw by blood.  You will also find affidavits relative to her death.

You are further advised that this child's mother name is Ida Ward on your approved rolls, and is a daughter of Allington and Sis or Phoebe Ward.

Yours Respectfully,
Carl Patterson.

---

7-NB-1532

Muskogee, Indian Territory, February 2, 1907.

Benson Thomas,
Soper, Indian Territory,

Dear Sir:

You are hereby advised that it appearing from the records of this office that your minor child, Sally Thomas, died prior to March 4, 1905, the Commissioner to the Five Civilized Tribes, on February 1, 1907, dismissed the application for her enrollment as a new born citizen by blood of the Choctaw Nation.

Respectfully,

Commissioner.

---

7-NB-1532

Muskogee, Indian Territory, February 4, 1907.

Benson Thomas,
Soper, Indian Territory.

Dear Sir:

Receipt is hereby acknowledged of the affidavits of Ida Thomas and Sweney Wallace to the birth of Sally Thomas, child of Benson and Ida Thomas, January 3, 1904; also affidavits of Benson Thomas and J. O. Nail to the death of Sally Thomas, a citizen of the Choctaw Nation which occurred January 24, 1905, and the same have been filed as evidence of death of said person.

Respectfully,

Commissioner.

---

7-NB-1532

Muskogee, Indian Territory, February 7, 1907.

Benson Thomas,
Soper, Indian Territory.

Dear Sir:

Receipt is hereby acknowledged of the affidavits of Ida Thomas and Sweney Wallace to the birth of Sally Thomas, child of Benson and Ida Thomas, January 3, 1904; also affidavits of Benson Thomas and J. O. Nail to the death of Sally Thomas, a citizen of the Choctaw Nation which occurred January 24, 1905, and the same have been filed as evidence of death of said child.

You are advised that on February 1, 1907, an order was entered dismissing the application for the enrollment of said child for the reason that she died prior to March 4, 1905.

Respectfully,

Commissioner.

Choc. New Born 1533
    William Watkins
    *(Birthdate not given.)*

**1533**

# NEW BORN
## CHOCTAW
### ENROLLMENT

WILLIAM WATKINS

As Citizen of the
CHOCTAW NATION
Act of Congress
Approved March 3, 1905

TRANSFERRED TO 7-1732
FEBRUARY 1, 1907

**1533**

*Choctaw* NEW BORN

*(Act March 3 1905)*
*William Watkins*

*Transferred to 7-1732*
*Feb. 1 1907*

Choc. New Born 1534
    Ida Bell Bennett
    (Born July 30, 1904)

1534

# NEW BORN
## CHOCTAW
### ENROLLMENT

IDA BELL BENNETT

(BORN JULY 30, 1904)

As Citizen of the
CHOCTAW NATION
Act of Congress
Approved March 3, 1905

R E F U S E D   FEBRUARY 15, 1907

ACTION APPROVED BY SECRETARY OF INTERIOR
MARCH 2, 1907

NOTICE OF DEPARTMENTAL ACTION FORWARDED
ATTORNEYS FOR CHOCTAW AND CHICKASAW NATIONS,
APRIL 12, 1907

NOTICE OF DEPARTMENTAL ACTION MAILED
APPLICANT.  APRIL 12, 1907

1534

---

BIRTH AFFIDAVIT.

## DEPARTMENT OF THE INTERIOR.
## COMMISSION TO THE FIVE CIVILIZED TRIBES.

---

IN RE APPLICATION FOR ENROLLMENT, as a citizen of the        Choctaw        Nation, of
Ida Bell Bennett        , born on the   30th   day of   July   , 1904

Name of Father:  William S. A. Bennett          a citizen of the   Choctaw   Nation.
Name of Mother:  Nancy Barthena Bennett        a citizen of the   Choctaw   Nation.

Postoffice        Marlow, Indian Territory.

---

174

# Applications for Enrollment of Choctaw Newborn
## Act of 1905   Volume XX

### AFFIDAVIT OF MOTHER.

UNITED STATES OF AMERICA, Indian Territory, ⎱
    Southern           DISTRICT. ⎰

I,   Nancy Barthena Bennett   , on oath state that I am  22    years of age and a citizen by   blood   , of the   Choctaw   Nation; that I am the lawful wife of   W. S. A. Bennett   , who is a citizen, by   marriage   of the   Choctaw Nation; that a   Female   child was born to me on  30th   day of   July   , 1904; that said child has been named   Ida Bell Bennett   , and was living March 4, 1905.

Mrs. Nancy Barthena Bennett

Witnesses To Mark:
⎰ David Willie, Jr.
⎱ Will Darnall

Subscribed and sworn to before me this  27th  day of   April   , 1905

Wm. A. Proctor<br>Southern District, I.T.   Notary Public.

---

### AFFIDAVIT OF ATTENDING PHYSICIAN OR MID-WIFE.

UNITED STATES OF AMERICA, Indian Territory, ⎱
    Southern           DISTRICT. ⎰

I,   Bettie Dunevant   , a   mid-wife   , on oath state that I attended on Mrs.   Nancy Barthena Bennett   , wife of   W. S. A. Bennett   on the 30th   day of   July   , 1904; that there was born to her on said date a   Female   child; that said child was living March 4, 1905, and is said to have been named  Ida Bell Bennett

Bettie Dunevant

Witnesses To Mark:
⎰ David Willie, Jr.
⎱ Will Darnall

Subscribed and sworn to before me this  27th  day of   April   , 1905

My Commission expires           Wm. A. Proctor<br>
February 16th, 1907.                   Notary Public.<br>
                                 Southern District, I.T.

---

BIRTH AFFIDAVIT.

DEPARTMENT OF THE INTERIOR,
# COMMISSIONER TO THE FIVE CIVILIZED TRIBES.

ENROLLMENT OF MINORS.   ACT OF CONGRESS, APPROVED APRIL 26, 1906.

IN RE APPLICATION FOR ENROLLMENT, as a citizen of the    Choctaw    Nation,
of    Ida Bell Bennett          , born on the  30    day of  July  , 1904

Name of Father: Wm. S. A. Bennett          a citizen of the ........................ Nation.
                                           Boen)
Name of Mother: Nancy Barthena Bennett (nee   a citizen of the   Choctaw   Nation.

Tribal enrollment of father  Court Claimant? Tribal enrollment of mother  Court Claimant

Postoffice    Addington, I. T. (?) C/o Jesse A. Boen

_____

AFFIDAVIT OF MOTHER.

UNITED STATES OF AMERICA, Indian Territory, ⎫
     Southern               District. ⎭

I,    Jesse A. Boen          , on oath state that I am    2    years of
age and  was  a citizen by    U. S. Court    , of the    Choctaw    Nation; that I
am ~~the lawful wife~~ **a full brother** of    Nancy Barthena Bennett    , who **was** ~~is~~ a
citizen, by    U. S. Court    of the    Choctaw    Nation; that a    female    child was
born to ~~me~~ **to her** on    30th    day of    July    , 1904 , that said child has been named
Ida Bell Bennett    , and was living March 4, 1906. & is now living.

Jessie[sic] A. Boen

WITNESSES TO MARK:
{

Subscribed and sworn to before me this  4th   day of    Feby  , 1907.

Lacey P. Bobo
Notary Public.

_____

176

7-NB-1534.                                                                      O.L.J.

### DEPARTMENT OF THE INTERIOR,
### COMMISSIONER TO THE FIVE CIVILIZED TRIBES.

-----

In the matter of the application for the enrollment of Ida Bell Bennett as a citizen by blood of the Choctaw Nation.

### D E C I S I O N.

It appears from the record herein that on April 29, 1905, application was made to the Commission to the Five Civilized Tribes for the enrollment of Ida Bell Bennett as a citizen by blood of the Choctaw Nation under the provisions of The Act of Congress approved March 3, 1905(33 Stats., 1060).

It further appears from the record herein that said applicant was born on July 30, 1904, and is the daughter of William S. A. Bennett, a non-citizen, and Nancy Barthena Bennett, who (as Nancy Barthena Bowen) was denied citizenship in the Choctaw Nation by the decree of the Choctaw and Chickasaw citizenship Court of November 29, 1904, in case No. 73 upon the Tishomingo Docket of said court.

I am, therefore, of the opinion that Ida Bell Bennett is not entitled to enrollment as a citizen of the Choctaw Nation and that her application for enrollment as such should be denied under the provisions of the Acts of Congress approved March 3, 1905 (33 Stats., 1060), and April 26, 1906 (34 Stats., 137), and it is so ordered.

Tams Bixby    Commissioner.

Muskogee, Indian Territory,
FEB 15 1907

---

7-NB-1534

**COPY**

Muskogee, Indian Territory, February 15, 1907.

William S. A. Bennett,
Marlow, Indian Territory.

Dear Sir:

Inclosed herewith you will find a copy of the decision of the Commissioner to the Five Civilized Tribes, rendered February 15, 1907, denying the application for the enrollment of Ida Bell Bennett as a citizen by blood of the Choctaw Nation.

The decision, with the record of proceedings in the case is this day transmitted to the Secretary of the Interior for review. The final decision of the Secretary will be made known to you as soon as this office is informed of the same.

Respectfully,

SIGNED   *Tams Bixby*
Commissioner

Incl. 7-NB-1534.
Registered.

---

7-NB-1534

**COPY**
Muskogee, Indian Territory, February 15, 1907.

Mansfield, McMurray & Cornish,
    Attorneys for Choctaw and Chickasaw Nations,
        South McAlester, Indian Territory.

Gentlemen:

Inclosed herewith you will find a copy of the decision of the Commissioner to the Five Civilized Tribes, rendered February 15, 1907, denying the application for the enrollment of Ida Bell Bennett as a citizen by blood of the Choctaw Nation.

The decision, with the record of proceedings in the case is this day transmitted to the Secretary of the Interior for review. The final decision of the Secretary will be made known to you as soon as this office is informed of the same.

Respectfully,

SIGNED   *Tams Bixby*
Commissioner.

Incl. 7-NB-1534.

---

**COPY**
Muskogee, Indian Territory, February 15, 1907.

The Honorable,
    The Secretary of the Interior:

Sir;-

There is transmitted herewith record of proceedings in the matter of the application for the enrollment of Ida Bell Bennett as a citizen by blood of the Choctaw Nation, including the decision of the Commissioner to the Five Civilized Tribes, dated February 15, 1907, denying said application.

Respectfully,

SIGNED   *Tams Bixby*

Commissioner.

2 Incl.

Through the
Commissioner of Indian Affairs.

---

Refer in reply to the following:                    **COPY**

DEPARTMENT OF THE INTERIOR,

Land.
17980-1907.              OFFICE OF INDIAN AFFAIRS.

WASHINGTON.

February 28, 1907.

The Honorable,
The Secretary of the Interior.

Sir:

There is enclosed report from Commissioner Bixby dated February 15, 1907, transmitting the record relative to the application of Ida Bell Bennett for enrollment as a citizen by blood of the Choctaw Nation, together with the Commissioner's decision of February 15, 1907, denying the application. The record has been examined and it is found that the Commissioner's decision is correct. Its approval is recommended.

Very respectfully,

C. F. Larrabee,

Acting Commissioner.

GAW-GH

---

# Applications for Enrollment of Choctaw Newborn
## Act of 1905   Volume XX

DEPARTMENT OF THE INTERIOR,

LRS                              WASHINGTON.                              O.K.
D.C. 12633-1907.
I.T.D.    6196,  6216,  6330,  6224-07.
          6236,  6246,  6266,  6272-07.
          6286,  6288,  6290,  6302-07.
          6306,  6478,  6480,  6486-07.
          6492,  6506,  6508,  6514-07.        March 2, 1907.
          6518,  6530,  6532,  6536-07.
          6672,  6674,  6688,  6692-07.
          6696,  6700,  6704,  6722-07.
          6724,  6734,  6736,  6740-07.
          6742,  6758,         6782-07.
                 6786,  6788,  6796-07.
          6798,  6806,  6816,  6826-07.
                        6828,  6830-07.

DIRECT.

Commissioner to the Five Civilized Tribes,
       Muskogee, Indian Territory.

Sir:

       Your decisions in the following Choctaw citizenship cases adverse to the applicants are hereby affirmed.  Copies of Indian Office letters submitting your reports and recommending that the decisions be affirmed are enclosed:

| Title of Case. | | Title of Your Letter of Transmittal. |
|---|---|---|
| Richard Floyd  , | (Freedman), | February 13, 1907. |
| Dave and Addie May Bailey, | (Freedman), | February 13, 1907. |
| Ardshia and Larce McKinney, | (Freedman), | February 16, 1907. |
| Nonie Cochran, | (Freedman), | February 13, 1907. |
| Mamey Cole and Liza Ellen Cole, | (Freedman), | February 14, 1907. |
| E. C. Seale, et al., | | February 14, 1907. |
| Hazell and Laveter Artry, | (Freedman), | February 14, 1907. |
| Nellie J. Gideon et al., | | December 28, 1906. |
| Emma and Evaline Jackson, | | February 14, 1907. |
| Ida Bell Bennett, | | February 15, 1907. |
| Memie Warner et al., | (Freedman), | February 14, 1907. |
| Katie Simpson et al., | | February 16, 1907. |
| Raymond Henry David, | | February 14, 1907. |
| Nancy T. Wilson et al, | (Miss. Choc.), | February 12, 1907. |
| J. H. Hill and Newton Hill, | | January   25, 1907. |

# Applications for Enrollment of Choctaw Newborn
## Act of 1905   Volume XX

| Title of Case. | | Title of Your Letter of Transmittal. |
|---|---|---|
| Flora Lee Spring | | January   25, 1907. |
| William Edgar and Oscar Jeffreys, | (Miss. Choc.), | February 11, 1907. |
| Celestine Pierce, | (Freedman), | February 13, 1907. |
| Hisk Cubit, | (Freedman), | February 13, 1907. |
| Lucretia Badnot et al., | | February 15, 1907. |
| Susan A. Baird, | | February 15, 1907. |
| William Allen Gee | (Miss. Choc.), | February 12, 1907. |
| Ella Williams, | (Freedman), | February 13, 1907. |
| Ida Colbert, | | February 12, 1907. |
| Mable Everidge, | (Freedman), | February 15, 1907. |
| Duckie May Mabrie, | (Freedman), | February 15, 1907. |
| Cornelious and Vaneda Riddle | (Freedman), | February 15, 1907. |
| Jimmie Lee Alexander, | (Freedman), | February 13, 1907. |
| Fred M. Patterson et al., | | February 15, 1907. |
| Ed Childers et al., | (Freedman), | February 12, 1907. |
| Lizzie Dennis, | (Freedman), | February 15, 1907. |
| Hellen D'Grace McMurty, | | February 12, 1907. |
| Mable Bailey and Susa Anna Bailey, | (Freedman), | February 13, 1907. |
| John Louis, | (Freedman), | February 15, 1907. |
| Amanda Mutchy, | (Freedman), | February 15, 1907. |
| Matt David et al., | | February 15, 1907. |
| Marjie Record, | (Freedman), | February 15, 1907. |
| Laura Henry, | (Freedman), | February 14, 1907. |
| Ollie Webster, | (Freedman), | February 15, 1907. |
| James McCall, | | February 15, 1907. |
| Nellie Elizabeth Kendrick, | (Freedman), | February 15, 1907. |
| Elwood Judy, | (Freedman), | February 15, 1907. |
| Oscar Brown, | (Freedman), | February 15, 1907. |
| Varna Verniti Bryant, | | February 13, 1907. |
| Richard R. Perry, | (Freedman), | February 15, 1907. |
| James Luke Tubbee, | (Miss. Choc.), | February 20, 1907. |
| Elmina Berryman, | (Miss. Choc.), | February 20, 1907. |
| Ethel Rogers, | (Miss. Choc.), | February 20, 1907. |

A copy hereof and all the papers in the above mentioned cases have been sent to the Indian Office.

Respectfully,
Jesse E. Wilson,
Assistant Secretary.

48 inc. and 96 inc.
for Ind. Of.

W. C. F.
3/3/07.

---

7-NB-1534

Muskogee, Indian Territory, April 12, 1907.

William S. A. Bennett,
Marlow, Indian Territory.

Dear Sir:

You are hereby advised that on March 2, 1907, the Secretary of the Interior affirmed the decision of this office of February 15, 1907, denying the application for the enrollment of Ida Bell Bennett as a citizen by blood of the Choctaw Nation.

Respectfully,

*Geo. D. Rodgers.*
ACTING   Commissioner.

---

7-NB-1534

Muskogee, Indian Territory, April 12, 1907.

Mansfield, McMurray & Cornish,
Attorneys for Choctaw and Chickasaw Nations,
South McAlester, Indian Territory.

Gentlemen:

You are hereby advised that on March 2, 1907, the Secretary of the Interior affirmed the decision of this office of February 15, 1907, denying the application for the enrollment of Ida Bell Bennett as a citizen by blood of the Choctaw Nation.

Respectfully,

*Geo. D. Rodgers.*
ACTING   Commissioner.

---

Muskogee, Indian Territory, May 1, 1905.

William S. A. Bennett,
    Marlow, Indian Territory.

Dear Sir:

Receipt is hereby acknowledged of the affidavits of Mrs. Nancy Barthena Bennett and Bettie Dunevant to the birth of Ida Bell Bennett, daughter of William S. A. and Nancy Barthena Bennett, July 30, 1904.

It is stated in the affidavit of the mother that she is a citizen by blood of the Choctaw Nation. If this is correct you are requested to state the name under which she was enrolled, the names of her parents, and if she has selected an allotment of the lands of the Choctaw or Chickasaw Nation please give her roll number as it appears upon her allotment certificate.

Respectfully,

Chairman.

---

Choc. New Born 1535
    Boe Isaac
    *(Birthdate not given.)*

————

**1535**

# NEW BORN
## CHOCTAW
### ENROLLMENT

BOE ISAAC

As Citizen of the
CHOCTAW NATION
Act of Congress
Approved March 3, 1905

TRANSFERRED TO 7-3059

FEBRUARY 18, 1907

G R A N T E D

## 1535

---

*Choctaw*

*(Act March 3 1905)*

*Boe Isaac*

*Transferred to 7-3059*
*Feb 18 1907*
*Granted*

---

Choc. New Born 1536
    Minnie Lee Morgan
    (Born Jan. 21, 1904)

---

1536

# NEW BORN
## CHOCTAW
### ENROLLMENT

MINNIE LEE MORGAN

(BORN JANUARY 21, 1904)

As Citizen of the
CHOCTAW NATION
Act of Congress
Approved March 3, 1905

184

## Applications for Enrollment of Choctaw Newborn
## Act of 1905   Volume XX

REFUSED FEBRUARY 7, 1907
COPY OF DECISION FORWARDED APPLICANT
FEBRUARY 7, 1907
COPY OF DECISION FORWARDED ATTORNEY FOR
APPLICANT. FEBRUARY 7, 1907
COPY OF DECISION FORWARDED ATTORNEYS FOR
CHOCTAW AND CHICKASAW NATIONS.
FEBRUARY 7, 1907
RECORD FORWARDED DEPARTMENT. FEBRUARY 7, 1907
ACTION APPROVED BY SECRETARY OF INTERIOR
FEBRUARY 28, 1907
NOTICE OF DEPARTMENTAL ACTION FORWARDED
ATTORNEYS FOR CHOCTAW AND CHICKASAW NATIONS,
APRIL 10, 1907
NOTICE OF DEPARTMENTAL ACTION FORWARDED
ATTORNEY FOR APPLICANT APRIL 10, 1907
NOTICE OF DEPARTMENTAL ACTION MAILED
APPLICANT. APRIL 10, 1907

## 1536

BIRTH AFFIDAVIT.

### DEPARTMENT OF THE INTERIOR.
### COMMISSION TO THE FIVE CIVILIZED TRIBES.

IN RE APPLICATION FOR ENROLLMENT, as a citizen of the        Choctaw        Nation, of
Minnie Lee        , born on the   21   day of   Jan  , 1904

Name of Father: Jas. C. Morgan                a citizen of the      U. S.      Nation.
Name of Mother: Annie Pearl                   a citizen of the   Choctaw    Nation.

Postoffice      Tussy I. Ter.

#### AFFIDAVIT OF MOTHER.

UNITED STATES OF AMERICA, Indian Territory, ⎱
   Southern                DISTRICT. ⎰

I,     Annie Pearl Morgan     , on oath state that I am   25     years of age and a
citizen by     Blood    , of the    Choctaw    Nation; that I am the lawful wife of   Jas.
C. Morgan        , who is a citizen, by ........................... of the        U. S.     Nation; that a
female     child was born to me on   21     day of    Jan     , 1904; that said child has
been named     Minnie Lee     , and was living March 4, 1905.

185

# Applications for Enrollment of Choctaw Newborn
## Act of 1905   Volume XX

Annie P. Morgan

Witnesses To Mark:

⟨SEAL⟩

Subscribed and sworn to before me this 26  day of  Apr  , 1905

H.G. Liston
Notary Public.

---

**AFFIDAVIT OF ATTENDING PHYSICIAN OR MID-WIFE.**

UNITED STATES OF AMERICA, Indian Territory, ⎫
    Southern            DISTRICT. ⎭

I,    J. I. Taylor    , a  Physician    , on oath state that I attended on
Mrs.  Annie Pearl   , wife of  Jas. C. Morgan    on the  21  day of  Jan   , 1904;
that there was born to her on said date a    Female    child; that said child was living
March 4, 1905, and is said to have been named   Minnie Lee

J.I. Taylor M.D.

Witnesses To Mark:

⟨SEAL⟩

Subscribed and sworn to before me this 25  day of  Apr  , 1905

H.G. Liston
Notary Public.

---

7-NB, 1536.
O.L.J.

## DEPARTMENT OF THE INTERIOR,
## COMMISSIONER TO THE FIVE CIVILIZED TRIBES.

---

In the matter of the application for the enrollment of Minnie Lee Morgan as a
citizen of the Choctaw Nation.

## D E C I S I O N.

It appears from the record herein that on May 1, 1905, application was made to
the Commissioner to the Five Civilized Tribes for the enrollment of Minnie Lee Morgan,
a citizen of the Choctaw Nation, under the provisions of The Act of Congress approved
March 3, 1905 (33 Stats., 1070).

It further appears from the record herein and from the records in the possession of this office that said applicant was born on January 21, 1904, and is the daughter of Jas. C. Morgan, a non citizen, and Amy[sic] P. Morgan who was denied citizenship in the Choctaw Nation by a decree of the Choctaw and Chickasaw citizenship court on March 21, 1904, in case No. 81, upon the McAlester docket of said court.

I am, therefore, of the opinion that the applicant, Minnie Lee Morgan, is not entitled to enrollment as a citizen of the Choctaw Nation either under the provisions of The Act of Congress approved March 3, 1905 (33 Stats., 1070) or under the Act of Congress approved April 26, 1906 (34 Stats., 137), and that her application for enrollment should be denied under the provisions of said Acts and it is so ordered.

Tams Bixby    Commissioner.

Dated at Muskogee, Indian Territory
this       FEB 7 1907

---

7-NB-1536

**COPY**

Muskogee, Indian Territory, February 7, 1907.

James C. Morgan,
     Tussy, Indian Territory.

Dear Sir:

Inclosed herewith you will find a copy of the decision of the Commissioner to the Five Civilized Tribes, rendered February 7, 1907, denying the application for the enrollment of Minnie Lee Morgan as a citizen of the Choctaw Nation.

The decision, with the record of proceedings in the case, is this day transmitted to the Secretary of the Interior for review. The final decision of the Secretary will be made known to you as soon as this office is informed of the same.

Respectfully,

SIGNED    *Tams Bixby*
Commissioner.

Registered.
Incl. 7-NB-1536

---

7-NB-1536

**COPY**

Muskogee, Indian Territory, February 7, 1907.

Cruce, Cruce & Bleakmore,
    Attorneys at law.
        Ardmore, Indian Territory.

Gentlemen:

    Inclosed herewith you will find a copy of the decision of the Commissioner to the Five Civilized Tribes, rendered February 7, 1907, denying the application for the enrollment of Minnie Lee Morgan as a citizen of the Choctaw Nation.

    The decision, with the record of proceedings in the case, is this day transmitted to the Secretary of the Interior for review. The final decision of the Secretary will be made known to you as soon as this office is informed of the same.

Respectfully,

SIGNED    *Tams Bixby*
          Commissioner.

Registered.
Incl. 7-NB-1536

---

7-NB-1536

**COPY**

Muskogee, Indian Territory, February 7, 1907.

Mansfield, McMurray & Cornish,
    Attorneys for Choctaw and Chickasaw Nations,
        South McAlester, Indian Territory.

Gentlemen:

    Inclosed herewith you will find a copy of the decision of the Commissioner to the Five Civilized Tribes, rendered February 7, 1907, denying the application for the enrollment of Minnie Lee Morgan as a citizen of the Choctaw Nation.

    The decision, with the record of proceedings in the case, is this day transmitted to the Secretary of the Interior for review. The final decision of the Secretary will be made known to you as soon as this office is informed of the same.

Respectfully,

SIGNED   *Tams Bixby*
Commissioner.

Incl. 7-NB-1536

---

**COPY**
Muskogee, Indian Territory, February 7, 1907.

The Honorable,
The Secretary of the Interior.

Sir:

There is transmitted herewith record of proceedings in the matter of the application for the enrollment of Minnie Lee Morgan as a citizen of the Choctaw Nation, including the decision of the Commissioner to the Five Civilized Tribes, dated February 7, 1907, denying said application.

Respectfully,

SIGNED

*Tams Bixby*
Commissioner.

2 Incl.

Through the
Commissioner of Indian Affairs.

---

DEPARTMENT OF THE INTERIOR,

D.C. 12433          OFFICE OF INDIAN AFFAIRS,

Land.                    WASHINGTON.                    February 23, 1907.
13709-1907

The Honorable,
The Secretary of the Interior.

Sir:

There is enclosed the record of proceedings in the matter of the application for the enrollment of Minnie Lee Morgan as a citizen of the Choctaw Nation, including the decision of the Commissioner to the Five Civilized Tribes, dated February 7, 1907, adverse to the applicant.

# Applications for Enrollment of Choctaw Newborn
## Act of 1905   Volume XX

The record shows that on May 1, 1905, application was made to the Commissioner to the Five Civilized Tribes for the enrollment of Minnie Lee Morgan as a citizen of the Choctaw Nation. The record further shows that the applicant was born on January 21, 1904, and is the daughter of Jas. C. Morgan, a non-citizen, and Amy[sic] P. Morgan, who was denied citizenship in the Choctaw Nation by decree of the Choctaw and Chickasaw Citizenship Court on March 21, 1904.

This case does not come within the Lulu West case, approved by the Department February 10, 1905, (I.T.D. 10353-04) as the applicant did not have a tribal status in 1896. Therefore by reason of the provisions of the Act of April 26, 1906 (34 Stat., L 137), the Office concurs in the decision of the Commissioner denying the enrollment of Minnie Lee Morgan as a citizen of the Choctaw Nation.

Very respectfully,<br>
C.F. Larrabee,

EBM.-D                                                    Acting Commissioner.

---

D.C. 12433                                                              J.P.

O.K.

DEPARTMENT OF THE INTERIOR,

I. T. D.                          WASHINGTON.
4902, 4966, 5000, 5010-1907.
5018, 5022, 5102, 5138-1907.
5140, 5142, 5174, 5180-1907.                      February 28, 1907.
L.R.S.
<u>DIRECT.</u>

Commissioner to the Five Civilized Tribes,
    Muskogee, Indian Territory.

Sir:-

Your decision in the follosing[sic] Choctaw citizenship cases adverse to the applicants are hereby affirmed. Copies of Indian Office letters submitting your reports and recommending that the decisions be affirmed are inclosed;

| Title of Case. | Date of Your Letter of Transmittal. |
|---|---|
| Agnes May Mills, | November 27, 1906. |
| Sarah Bailiff (Freedman), | January   18, 1907. |
| Vero Wootten (Freedman), | January   26, 1907. |
| Floyed Goodson, | January   17, 1907. |
| Omer H. and Cecil R. Marr, | January    9, 1907. |
| Charles Walter Morrow, | January    9, 1907. |
| Maud and Elzy Turner, (Miss. Choc.) | January   21, 1907. |

# Applications for Enrollment of Choctaw Newborn
## Act of 1905   Volume XX

| | |
|---|---|
| Willie Colbert et al, | January 30, 1907. |
| Johny Vails, | February 5, 1907. |
| Maggie Francis Carroll, | January 16, 1907. |
| Minnie Lee Morgan, | February 7, 1907. |
| Robert Nelson, (Johnson?) | January 26, 1907. |

A copy hereof and all the papers in the above mentioned cases have been sent to the Indian Office.

Respectfully,

Jesse E. Wilson,

12 inc. and 24 inc.                    Assistant Secretary.
for Ind. Of.

AFMc
-------------
3-1-07.

-----------

7-NB-1536

Muskogee, Indian Territory, April 10, 1907.

James C. Morgan,
        Tussy, Indian Territory.

Dear Sir:

You are hereby advised that on February 28, 1907, the Secretary of the Interior affirmed the decision of this office of February 7, 1907, denying the application for the enrollment of Minnie Lee Morgan as a citizen of the Choctaw Nation.

Respectfully,

*Geo. D. Rodgers.*

Acting Commissioner.

-----------

7-NB-1536

Muskogee, Indian Territory, April 10, 1907.

Cruce, Cruce & Bleakmore,
Attorneys at Law,
Ardmore, Indian Territory.

Gentlemen:

You are hereby advised that on February 28, 1907, the Secretary of the Interior affirmed the decision of this office of February 7, 1907, denying the application for the enrollment of Minnie Lee Morgan as a citizen of the Choctaw Nation.

Respectfully,

*Geo. D. Rodgers.*

Acting Commissioner.

———————

7-NB-1536

Muskogee, Indian Territory, April 10, 1907.

Mansfield, McMurray & Cornish,
Attorneys for Choctaw and Chickasaw Nations,
South McAlester, Indian Territory.

Gentlemen:

You are hereby advised that on February 28, 1907, the Secretary of the Interior affirmed the decision of this office of February 7, 1907, denying the application for the enrollment of Minnie Lee Morgan as a citizen of the Choctaw Nation.

Respectfully,

*Geo. D. Rodgers.*
Acting Commissioner.

———————

# Applications for Enrollment of Choctaw Newborn
## Act of 1905 Volume XX

Muskogee, Indian Territory, May 6, 1905.

Cruce, Cruce & Bleakmore,
Attorneys at Law,
Ardmore, Indian Territory.

Gentlemen:

Receipt is hereby acknowledged of your letter without date enclosing affidavits of Annie P. Morgan and J. I. Taylor to the birth of Minnie Lee Morgan, daughter of James C. and Annie Pearl Morgan, January 21, 1904.

It is stated in the affidavit of the mother that she is a citizen by blood of the Choctaw Nation. If this is correct you are requested to state the name under which she was enrolled, the names of her parents, and if she has selected an allotment of the lands of the Choctaw or Chickasaw Nation please give her roll number as it appears upon her allotment certificate.

Respectfully,

Commissioner in Charge.

---

Muskogee, Indian Territory, May 31, 1905.

James C. Morgan,
Tussy, Indian Territory.

Dear Sir:

Referring to the application for the enrollment of your child, Minnie Lee Morgan, it is stated in the affidavit of the mother that she is a citizen by blood of the Choctaw Nation, and if this is correct you are requested to state the name under which she was enrolled, the names of her parents, and if she has selected an allotment of the lands of the Choctaw or Chickasaw Nation, please give her roll number as it appears upon her allotment certificate.

This matter should receive immediate attention in order that proper disposition may be made of the application for the enrollment of Minnie Lee Morgan.

Respectfully,

[sic]

---

# Applications for Enrollment of Choctaw Newborn
## Act of 1905   Volume XX

Robberson, I. Ty.
January 22, 1907.

Commissioner to Five Tribes,
Muskogee, I. Ty.

Dear Sir:

Relative to the enrollment, as a citizen of the Choctaw Nation, of Minnie Lee Morgan, minor child of Jas C. Morgan and Amy[sic] P. Morgan you are advised that I have seen the mother of the applicant and she states that she has never been approved as a citizen of the Choctaw or Chickasaw Nations[sic], and that she is what is commonly known as a "Court Claimant".

She states further that her application for citizenship in the Choctaw Nation was made through her father D. B. Vernon.

The data in this case is returned herewith.

Respectfully,
Andrew J. Gardenhire.

---

Choc. New Born 1537
    Aylene Camp
    (Born Dec. 31, 1902)

    Jacket empty.

    See N.B. 1538.

---

Choc. New Born 1538
    Aylene Camp
    *(Born December 31, 1902)*

**1538**

# NEW BORN
## CHOCTAW
### ENROLLMENT

AYLENE CAMP

As Citizen of the
CHOCTAW NATION
Act of Congress
Approved March 3, 1905

DISMISSED MARCH 4, 1907

It appearing from the within affidavits that Aylene Camp for whose enrollment application was made under the Act of Congress Approved March 3, 1905, (33 Stat., 1070), died May 16, 1904, I am of the opinion that the application for the enrollment of Aylene Camp as a new born citizen of the Choctaw Nation, should be, and the same is, dismissed.

Tams Bixby   Commissioner.

Muskogee, Indian Territory.
MAR 4- 1907

BIRTH AFFIDAVIT.
### DEPARTMENT OF THE INTERIOR.
## COMMISSION TO THE FIVE CIVILIZED TRIBES.

IN RE APPLICATION FOR ENROLLMENT, as a citizen of the   Choctaw   Nation, of Aylene Camp   , born on the   31$^{st}$   day of   December   , 1902

Name of Father: Joseph A Camp   a citizen of the   Choctaw   Nation.
Name of Mother: Allie Camp   a citizen of the   Choctaw   Nation.

Postoffice   Paoli I.T.

# Applications for Enrollment of Choctaw Newborn
## Act of 1905   Volume XX

AFFIDAVIT OF MOTHER.

UNITED STATES OF AMERICA, Indian Territory, ⎫
Southern                    DISTRICT. ⎭

I,   Allie Camp   , on oath state that I am   33   years of age and a citizen by
Marriage   , of the   Choctaw   Nation; that I am the lawful wife of   Joseph A
Camp   , who is a citizen, by blood   of the   Choctaw   Nation; that a
female   child was born to me on   31$^{st}$   day of   December   , 1902; that said
child has been named Aylene Camp   , and ~~was living March 4, 1905~~. *died May 16 1904*

Allie Camp

Witnesses To Mark:

{

Subscribed and sworn to before me this   11$^{th}$   day of   April   , 1905

JE Williams
Notary Public.

_____

AFFIDAVIT OF ATTENDING PHYSICIAN OR MID-WIFE.

UNITED STATES OF AMERICA, Indian Territory, ⎫
Southern                    DISTRICT. ⎭

I,   Lottie Wallace   , a   midwife   , on oath state that I attended on
Mrs.   Allie Camp   , wife of   Joseph A Camp   on the   31$^{st}$   day of   December ,
1902; that there was born to her on said date a   female   child; that said child ~~was
living March 4, 1905~~, and is said to have been named
*died May 16 1904*

Lottie Wallace
Witnesses To Mark:

{

Subscribed and sworn to before me this   11$^{th}$   day of   April   , 1905

JE Williams
Notary Public.

_____

## Applications for Enrollment of Choctaw Newborn
## Act of 1905   Volume XX

Muskogee, Indian Territory, April 17, 1905.

Joseph A. Camp,
　　Paoli, Indian Territory.

Dear Sir:

Receipt is hereby acknowledged of the affidavits of Allie Camp and Lottie Wallace to the birth of Aylene Camp, daughter of joseph A. and Allie Camp, December 31, 1902.

It appears that this child died May 16, 1904 and under the provisions of the act of Congress approved March 3, 1905, the Commission is authorized to receive applications for enrollment of children born to enrolled citizens by blood of the Choctaw and Chickasaw Nations between September 25, 1902, and March 4, 1905, and living on said latter date. You will therefore see that the Commission is without authority to enroll your child Aylene Camp.

Respectfully,

Chairman.